GEMS FOR THE JOURNEY

BOB COLE

<u>Gems for the Journey</u>

Published by Cole & Company

Tallahassee, Florida

ISBN 0-615-12827-0

Cover Design By D. E. Matthews
Page Design By Melissa Matthews

Ordering Information
www.gemsforthejourney.com
Info@gemsforthejourney.com

Printed by Rose Printing,
Tallahassee, Florida

DEDICATED

To my lovely wife

Betty,

a gift from God

and a precious gem

who has

enriched the journey.

ACKNOWLEDGEMENTS

I wish to express my utmost gratitude to my Lord and Savior, and Provider, Jesus, who spared me and saved me and gave me a testimony, a purpose, and ample courage for the journey.

To the dear persons who encouraged, inspired, and challenged me to compile <u>Gems for the Journey</u>, namely Pastor Mark, my wife, Betty and our wonderful son, Robert and his wife Diana.

To the typists: Betty, my precious daughter-in-law Diana, and Classie Scott of Champions for Life.

A special thanks to the talented Cindy Graves, who did most of the editing. Any errors are mine.

To all the pastors and fellow believers who shared their lives with me, I readily say, thank you again and again for your teaching, your training, your tutoring and your truth you ministered to me along the way.

Last, but certainly not least, is the artistry and expertise of Donald and Melissa Matthews who put it all together. An overflowing "thanks" to both of you.

Bob Cole

FORWARD

This is an excellent read. Bob Cole shares many of his experiences as a teammate counselor in those early years and later as a Platform Guest in the Weekend of Champions. It will serve as excellent background reading for those looking for inspirational stories and ideas.

It is classic Bob Cole. Not a dry theologian or lofty scholar, but an excellent front-line witness in the toughest situations.

He has served as a volunteer - paying his own way to countless Weekend of Champions. These stories are some of his best material used in speaking and elsewhere.

I have read and read again many of these brief stories because most are complete within one page. Just open the book and Bob is up in your face with an interesting story or just an idea of interest. He has a good sense of humor and tells a story well. His style goes over well in prison and also in the free world. On a plane, between meetings, in church, or on your bedside table, Bob's book can fit into your life successfully.

It is a book about life in general with a prison ministry flavor. Thanks Bob, for your time and talent donated to the Lord and for this book as well!

Bill Glass

FROM THE AUTHOR

The sole purpose of this book is to bring honor and glory to the God I know, and love and serve, even the Lord Jesus. The opinions, innuendoes, thoughts, and words are mine alone. I represent no group, organization, or political party. I represent only one person, the Lord Jesus, Himself.

The Greeks had a word for Him. They called Him the monoganace, the only one, the one of a kind, the unique Christ. He is much, much more!

There are many names for our Lord. His word for us, the most gratifying we could ever hear is "forgiven." He truly is, "The Ineffable Tetra Grammaton."

I receive no monetary gain from this book. Any profit from the sales goes to a designated non profit organization to share the gospel.

A lot of what is written are some "gems" I have discovered on this long exciting journey with God. The best part of the book is what He has revealed. Most of the "gems" came from God's own treasure house, His word. Be mindful of the ultimate, most precious "gem" of all the ages, "The Pearl of Great Price."

I have attempted to give proper credit to the original authors. A great number of tidbits in this book were first written by a fellow named "unknown."

Enjoy this book and remember . . . it is for God's glory.

CONTENTS

A Journey 1
In The Beginning 3
The Indispensable Book 5
Two Treasures 7
Just A Game Of Poker 8
Don't Lose The Luster 10
Help-Meet 11
Your Gun Is Loaded 12
A Spoonful 13
Jesus Is Enough 14
The World Needs To Know 15
A Threat 17
Salvation (Set Free, Rescued) 18
Commitment 19
Deacon's Meeting 21
Worship 22
Boat Story 23
Credit 25
Never Passes Away 26
Believe In Your Heart 27
Never Too Old 28
Getting Personal 29
A 25 Year Old Drunk 30
What's All This Fuss About Giving? 31
Money Talks 33
I Can't Remember 34
The Pits 35
The Fervent Prayer 37
No Patching 38
First Day of Spring 39
Easter 40
Naked 41

CONTENTS

No Options 42
Home Grown Sayings 43
Winsome 44
Attitude 45
Choice of Attitude 46
Self Esteem 47
Zacchaeus 48
Father Image 50
Correct Words 51
Pungent Activity Verbs 52
Faith Came Singing 53
Faith (A Gamble?) 54
Wisdom Personified 56
If I Should Live 58
Planned Versus Canned 59
Three P's 60
Agape 61
Our Theme Song 62
Double Tough 63
Disciple 64
What Is Number One? 66
Nameless People 68
Last Best Hope 69
"I Will Return" 70
It's Late 71
Truth 72
Custer's Last Words 73
Very Odd Definitions 74
Home Grown Definitions 75
2 – Number Sermon 76
Priorities 77
Mary Had A Little Lamb 78

CONTENTS

Not Much To Give 79
What Is Christmas? 80
Magic of Christmas 81
Twas The Day After Christmas 82
Baseball Chapel 83
Three Strikes – You're Out! 84
Christian Golfer 85
One Ball – One Life 86
God Given Life Themes 87
Salient Truths 90
Proofs For The Word 91
New Year – New Creature 92
A Day's Journey 94
Questionable Motives 96
Good Common Sense 97
Barriers 97
Saturday Was Different 98
Quiet Time 100
Invaluable 101
An Open Letter 102
This Year 104
The Way 105
A Loving Fellowship 106
All Day A Prayer 108
Bluegrass Miracles – Henry Holley 109
Bluegrass Miracles – The Crusade 110
Ponder This 113
Bric-A-Brac 114
Two Ends 117
Why Go To Prisons 119
Letters From Inmates 120

CONTENTS

Thirty Years In Prison 121
Is It Worth It 123
Pure Conjecture .125
Weekend of Champions 127
Coordinators 128
Platform Guests 129
Teammates 131
No Attack – No Defense 132
Logistics 133
Home Counts 134
Jailhouse Days .135
A Free Crime 136
Visit In Psycho Ward 136
What I Tell Inmates 137
No Game Playing 140
Waupun 141
Death Row 143
Until You've Been Arrested 144
Alabama Death Row 145
Scooter 146
He Keeps Telling 147
Amazing Grace 149
Walla Wonders 151
Glad I was In Prison 153
You Go First 154
Donald Lykins .155
George Joslin .157
Can't Go Home Again 158
Heroes Of Faith 159
The Finest Hour 161
Ineffable Tetra Grammaton 162
Enough Is Enough 163

GEMS
FOR THE
JOURNEY

A JOURNEY

Greetings in the Name of our Savior, The Lord Jesus.

Christianity is a journey, not a destination - a journey with Jesus - a Christ Way. In this life no one has arrived. Paul said, "I count not that I have apprehended." Incidentally, the only person we can be certain of improving on this journey is our self. We are all travelers from "birth to death." We travel between the eternities. The scripture says, "we are sojourners in a foreign country." While traveling on this journey with Jesus and His followers, I discovered that I do not know everything, but what I do know, I know for certain.

> I know that Jesus loves me.
> I know that Jesus loves everyone equally.

There are three old faithful friends in the scriptures, and they all begin with, "And I know."

> "And I know that all things work together for good for them that love God, and are called according to His purposes."
>
> Romans 8:28

> "And I know whom I have believed and am persuaded that He is able to keep that which I have committed unto Him against that day."
>
> 2 Timothy 1:12

"And I know that whatsover God doeth, it shall be forever. Nothing can be put to it, nor anything taken from it . . ."

Eccl. 3:14

Who said there isn't much about eternal security in the Old Testament? And finally, the best, "And I know — is:

And I know that I am paid for - I can soar to the Heavens with the Lord. It doesn't make any difference what happens, I am going to be with Jesus for all eternity!

He hit a home run with the bases loaded.

Praise the Lord!

IN THE BEGINNING

Many wonderful stories begin, "Once upon a time" - a great start, but look at how God began His story. In His powerful, life giving drama of redemption, He said, "In the beginning, God." Mere man could never have thought of this. It could only have been God.

Just as in eternity past, God the Father, God the Son, and God the Holy Spirit made the very first covenant. "Let us make mankind in our own image." Ephesians 1:4 bears out they also agreed to "re-make man in their own image." Any being who can say, "I am, I ought, I think" is made in the image of God.

Many scientists have as their first premise, "How did the world begin?" Billions and billions of dollars are spent on research and exploration. Scientists have made some exciting discoveries. They sent a giant satellite with a telescope named Hubble aboard into space, and it had to be adjusted to focus properly. They wanted to explore some "black holes" in the universe. Someday, they probably will find through those "black holes" more universes with more "black holes." There will be great consternation.

God would want us to be kind and considerate and very careful about judging and merely say, "In the beginning God created the Heaven and Earth." Ex Nihilo (Out of Nothing).

* * * God said it (in His Word)
* * * I believe it (in my heart)
* * * That settles it forever (for me)

Whether I, or anyone else believes it, it is still settled.

"The Lord's wisdom formed the earth, His understanding established all the universe and space."

Proverbs 3:19

THE INDISPENSABLE BOOK

Woodrow Wilson once said, "When you have read the Bible, you will know that it is the Word of God, because you will have found it the key to your own heart, your own happiness, and your own duty." Sir William Blackstone, in his famous commentaries on the laws of England, wrote, "The Bible has always been regarded as part of the Common Law of England." John Milton said, "In all literature, there is nothing that compares with the Bible." John Adams commented, "The Bible is the best book in the world." Matthew Arnold observed, "To the Bible men will return. And why? Because they cannot do without it."

There has never been any other book like the Bible. Other books must be changed, to meet the changing times and new truths discovered, but the Bible has never had to be changed and will never need to be. A revision of the language has sometimes been made in order to express its message, more clearly. But to revise its language does not mean that its message is different. We do not need a new Bible. We need a new determination to read the Bible we have.

"God has given us a book that tells us of our sins and of His provision for meeting the spiritual needs of our lives. This Book is sufficient, and will continue to be in ages to come. Men may deny this Book. Some have tried to destroy it. But in the last day they will find themselves being judged according to the laws and principles laid down in it. The Lord said, 'He that rejecteth me, and receiveth not my words, hath one that judgeth him; the Words that I have spoken, the same shall judge him in the last day.' (John 12:48). Friend, what is your attitude toward God's word?"

(Virtrus L. Buzbee)

The Bible is a good meeting place with God. We can hear the voice of God through the Word of God.

*"No one ever graduates from
Bible study until he meets
the author face to face."*

E. T. Harris

*"Nobody ever outgrows scripture:
the Book widens and deepens
with the years."*

Charles H. Spurgeon

TWO TREASURES

"Just think! Though I did nothing to deserve it, and though I am the most useless Christian there is, yet I was the one chosen for this special joy of telling others the Glad News of the endless treasures available to them in Christ;"

Ephesians 3:8 Living Letters

"Since you became alive again, so to speak, when Christ arose from the dead, now set your sights on the rich treasures and joys awaiting you in heaven . . ."

Colossians 3:1 Living Letters

JUST A GAME OF POKER

Life is just a game of poker;

Happiness is the pot.

Fate deals us all five cards, and

We play whether we like it or not.

Some are dealt with a pat hand,

Others with only a pair.

Some are beat before the draw, and it

Doesn't always seem on the square.

Me, I was just a gambler of misfortune.

I took to drinking and sin.

Seemed like I was always waiting –

For a ship, that would never come in!

But my ship did come in!

That is the ship of eternal life and

Heaven with all its joys.

I got to meet the Captain of that ship

And His name is Jesus!

Bob Cole

DON'T LOSE THE LUSTER!!

Sometimes we lose sight of the value of our Christianity, and when we do, we lose the luster — and we steal from our own lives. So, here are some luster restoring ideas we can use right now . . . and every day from now on:

* Understand that anything, no matter how exciting in the beginning, *will grow, may not grow, will grow stale,* in time if we are not careful. Dead things decay. Only live things grow — feed our faith — starve our doubts.

* Keep in mind that fighting off staleness in our Christianity is a daily job. There is something WE can — something WE must — do every day in order to keep vitality — "LIVE THE PART"

* See "God's Big Picture" — see our role in relation to God's whole scheme of things. Our service to Him is ALL IMPORTANT.

* Finally, keep developing ourselves, our service, and all that we do, through the eyes of that most important person — *Jesus!* And remember,

Don't Ever Lose the Luster!!

1963

HELP-MEET
(OUR SECOND HIGHEST PRIORITY)

In the second chapter of Genesis, God said He would make a helpmeet for Adam. Helpmeet means suitable, but much, much more.

Most men I know would gladly give up not just one rib, but many of their ribs for their helpmeet. It seems they already have our hearts. Suitable? You bet! One of God's greatest inventions.

Helpmeets complement and fulfill a man's life. We could use hundreds of adjectives to describe our mates, and after a half-century, I'm still blessed and grateful beyond mere words for the very best part of my life, my helpmeet.

The meaning of "God's peace" is bound together like marriage. No wonder we are called the "Bride of Christ." Praise the Lord for helpmeets!

Christianity is an all-the-time thing, not just a once-in-awhile thing. So is marriage!

God's ideal has always been: one man, one woman, and one family for life!

Helpmeets are also "called" beside their mates in kingdom endeavors. What a tremendous reinforcement and encouragement. "Yoked" together and "yoked" with Jesus. A WINNING COMBINATION!

YOUR GUN IS LOADED

As a very "young in the faith" Christian, I wanted others to know our Savior. I asked my young preacher to go with me on many occasions to share Christ with folks. Many of those people trusted Christ. It was like "shooting fish in a rain barrel." One Saturday afternoon I drove over to our little church to pick up the pastor. I had made a date to see a man who owned a service station. The pastor said he had a deacons meeting scheduled for that evening. He backed out of our meeting. I insisted on his going, but to no avail. He seemed a little disturbed and he said, "Your gun is loaded, you go." I went. I quoted some of the same scriptures that my pastor had shared. I really overstayed my visit. The fellow seemed interested, but that's as far as it went. I went home very disgusted and knew I had failed miserably.

Two evenings later as I was coming home from work, I saw this man at his station. He was kneeling down and locking his gasoline pumps. I drove right up to him. He said, "Bob, we're closed." I told him I did not need gas, but asked, "Have you thought any more of what we were talking about?" He said, "I haven't been able to think about anything else." I asked him if he was ready to trust the Lord. Kneeling down again by his gasoline pumps, he trusted Christ. He was in church the next Sunday. God always honors His word.

A SPOONFUL

On this journey with Jesus, I have listened intently to many learned men and women. I am like the poet, who wondered how folks of all sizes and shapes could be so knowledgeable. How could such small heads hold so much?

Yet even the most brilliant people have a very miniscule amount of the entire world's knowledge.

Let's say that all the oceans of the world are like all the knowledge in existence. Each one of us hopefully has about a spoonful. Everything in the spoon is all ocean, but it is not all the oceans. It appears that some of us try to read into some of God's Word that which was never there. We have probably missed some of the simplest truths. We might want to kick ourselves at the end of the journey. But, if we with just a spoonful give it our very best shot, and an honest college try, through God's grace we will hear from that great ocean of knowledge:

"Well Done Thy Good
And Faithful Servant"

JESUS IS ENOUGH

Jesus is absolutely and positively enough! He needs no assistance in His plan of salvation. David did not pray in the 51st Psalm, "Restore unto me the joy of <u>my</u> salvation," he said, "Restore unto me the joy of <u>Thy</u> salvation".

Some supposedly learned people have said, "Yes, Jesus, but much, much more." If they mean we should be yoked with Jesus in service, that is one thing. If they even hint or imply in any form that Jesus needed something else to effect salvation, then this does not border on blasphemy, it is blasphemy! "Yes, Jesus, but much, much more," has a different drummer with an uncertain sound. The first author of this statement was kicked out of heaven with his angels.

This hideous statement implies that God is not brilliant enough or powerful enough to save completely, without some help. Phooey! God is all powerful. "The blood of Jesus cleanses us from all sin." Not the blood and something else!

Any add-ons to Jesus are merely means to raise money or to get members to buy a lie. If the above statement seems rather crass, I would advise anyone to check it out thoroughly. Get the Holy Spirit's appraisal, and we will all say,

"Jesus Is Enough"

THE WORLD NEEDS TO KNOW

The world needs to know the right answer to a question Jesus asked His disciples and all of us. This question is demanding, life-changing, haunting, and vital. It needs the correct answer! He asked His disciples and all people everywhere, "Who do men say that I am?" Incidentally, we not only bet our lives, but we bet our eternities on this question. We cannot afford to lose!

History says Jesus was a baby boy born in a stable in Bethlehem, placed in a manger filled with straw and kept warm by a donkey's breath. Straw is very common. Donkeys aren't too regal. He grew up to be a carpenter's helper. Jesus says of Himself, "I am the way, the truth, and the life. No one comes to the Father except by me." Christians say, "He took our sins in His own body on the tree." He satisfied all of God's demands. He became our vicarious sacrifice and made us acceptable to God. He is the way to be walked! The truth to be told! The life to be lived! And the Light to be lit!

God the Father walked down the backstairs of heaven with a baby in His arms and placed that baby in Bethlehem's barn. That baby grew up to be the perfect God-man who was tempted in all points as you and I, yet without sin. Then Jesus voluntarily gave His life. He laid it down. We have to get this point straight. Nobody "took" Jesus' life. He laid it down for people worldwide and a fool like me. but the cross couldn't hold him! Death could not hold him! The grave couldn't hold him! He came out of there just like He said He would, and He cannot lie. He is even now at the right hand of God the Father forever making intercession for our sins. . . and best of all, He is coming back to get us one of these days. He said so!

He is very plain and specific about whom He is coming back to get. The Bible says, "To as many as received Jesus, to them He gave the right to become the children of God, even to those who believe on His name." This is the key. "Receive" . . . we must receive Jesus, not just believe about Him, but receive him into our lives as Savior and Lord. It is very simple. Merely tell God that you are sorry for your sins, ask His forgiveness, and ask Jesus to come into your heart. Many, many before have done just that. You can do it! It might take some courage, but you can do it! You will become more eternal than the moon and the sun and the stars! God help you in your decision. He will become your Savior and your Lord. This is the correct answer to the question Jesus asked.

A THREAT

Sometimes believers are a threat to non-believers. Many non-believers are firmly entrenched in their beliefs. Often their positions are untenable, but they are still positions. Our words and deeds are a real threat to their entire existence. They ask themselves, "What if this guy is right? That will make me wrong."

We need to realize that people without Christ are prisoners; that is, prisoners of their own egos, or prisoners of the world system. Jesus said it best, "You are of your father, the devil."

Often they become genuinely irritated with us. At this point we need guidance from the Holy Spirit. We must be careful not to "bruise the fruit." We need to be winsome.

In sales we do not "make" people buy anything from us, rather we make them "want to." We cannot "make" people trust Christ. We can only make them "want to."

Jesus said, "For the Holy Spirit shall teach you in the same hour what you ought to say." Luke 12:12. One of the gifts of the Holy Spirit, . . . "He shall teach you all things, and bring all things to your remembrance whatever I have said unto you." John 14:26

God will do all of the convicting. He will do all the conversion. He will cause all the confession.

We are concerned, we confront, we convince. Now our task is over. God takes charge. The results are His!

John 8:32

SALVATION (SET FREE, RESCUED)

Share Christ in the power of the Holy Spirit, and leave the results up to God. We are concerned about people. We go to people and confront people with the gospel. We try to convince the best way we know how. At this point the Holy Spirit takes over.

* HE does all the convicting.
* HE does all the conversion.
* HE causes the confession.

None of us can "save" anyone! Only God can do this! Our theme song, Col. 1:28, 29 (Living Letters) reads, "So everywhere we go, we talk about Jesus to all who will listen, warning them and teaching them, the best way we know how. We want to present each one to God, perfect because of what Christ has done for each of them. This is my work and I can only do it because Christ's mighty energy is at work within me."

Some people say they are under a lot of pressure when they witness. Anything repeated under pressure tends to groove itself into permanence. The more times we share, the less pressure and better performance. Incidentally, in order to improve our performance in anything, we must first improve in the way we see ourselves. We need to be at our best, because it is so vital! God Was At His Best When He Saved Us!

COMMITMENT

Commitment is an essential part of our makeup. It's like a starter for an engine, and it needs to be fueled to keep going. It is similar to "putting feet on our prayers." We could make an equation for a personal worker. P.W. = C. + A. The "C" stands for commitment, and the "A" stands for ability. They are usually in about this ratio: 99% commitment plus 1% ability equals a personal worker. Sometimes, just our availability will satisfy the Lord. He will supply all that is needed to accomplish the task.

There are some memorable commitments recorded in scripture: Jacob after his dream at Bethel, Abraham under the stars, Ruth who said, "Your God shall be my God. Wherever thou goest I will go;" or Isaiah saying, "Here am I Lord, send me," or Paul on his Damascus journey, "Lord, what will you have me do?" Note that all of these commitments were at a real time and at a real place. Jacob had to go back to Bethel, where he piled up the rocks and renewed his commitment. Paul referred to the Damascus road experience often. All of the above-mentioned saints at one time had to stand up and tell God He could count on them."

This is real commitment for them and us; not to a Sunday School teacher, or a pastor, or anyone else, but to the God who loves us!

In the must-read book, _The World's Greatest Salesman,_ there are three excellent sayings: 1) "Failure will never overtake me if my determination to succeed is strong enough." 2) "I will form good habits and become their slaves." 3) "I will greet each new day with love in my heart."

One meaning for agape is "Unconditional, willful, intelligent commitment," says Dr. Robert McMillan.

Commitment is always under-girded and underwritten by integrity. Integrity means, "I will do what I say I will do."

The unchanging word of God says, "And I know that whatsover God doeth, it shall be forever."

Perfect Commitment!

DEACONS' MEETING —
"WE NEVER DID IT LIKE THIS BEFORE"

At a deacons' meeting not too long ago, there was a "tepid" discussion concerning the process of land acquisition and building new and much larger facilities. Finally, it came out: "We never did it like this before." The deacons began choosing sides. Then an older deacon rose and said, "Dear hearts, if we open a quarrel between the past and the present, we most assuredly will lose the future." The day was won for the Lord's vision! Everyone got on board.

Praise The Lord!

WORSHIP

Some years ago the meaning of worship became the subject of a lively discussion. This happened in a church newcomer's class. Many interpretations and meanings were espoused. Some renditions were philosophical. Some were very religious. Platitudes abounded. One member of the class even explained the literal meaning, as trading by ships, etc.

After much discussion a very small, frail, older lady arose, and said, "Bob, Doesn't worship just mean, Lord, I love you." Wow!

I invited her to come forward to teach the class. She declined. You see, she had already taught us.

BOAT STORY (LUKE 8:22 - 24)

We are deeply indebted to Dr. Luke for his account of the journey of Jesus and his disciples across Lake Tiberius (Galilee), and the sudden storm.

This is a very vivid and symbolic experience that all can relate to. Storms of life are part and parcel to our very existence. When we hear such words as cancer, incurable, bad wreck, fatal and such, our list of priorities shrinks dramatically.

Jesus and his disciples were in a boat that they could not bail out of fast enough. In fact, Jesus was sleeping in the back of the boat. The disciples said, "We are perishing!" All of us can identify with this.

They woke up Jesus and he "took care of business." We are familiar with the rest of the story.

When the storms in our lives occur, there are three points we need to remember:

1. Your boat is not going to sink!
2. The storm is not going to last forever!
3. The best point is this: Jesus did say,
   "Let us go over to the other side."
   He did not say, "Let's go out into the
   lake and drown."

What Jesus says is in concrete, it's solid!

Isn't it amazing that the storm did not awaken Jesus. The tossing boat, the waves, and the lightning did not wake Him. But, when one of His children was scared and hurting and touched Him, then He came awake and "took care of business." He still does! He calmed the waves and their hearts. Sometimes we have to go through the thorn room to get to the throne room.

Note: those were believers in the boat with Jesus. We need to be certain He is also in our boat. In the storms of life we need His precious presence.

Even in our darkest hour, God always breaks thru with his brightest hope, JESUS!

"Other books were given
for our information.
The Bible was given
for our transformation."

Anonymous

CREDIT

A raggedly old bum was panhandling at his favorite corner in a small town. A young preacher approached him and took out his billfold. The preacher wished to give the bum a dollar, but all he had was a five-dollar bill. He told the old bum he would catch him later. The bum mumbled something. The preacher asked him, "What did you say?" He answered, "You would be surprised at how much money I have lost giving people credit."

Credit can be good and credit can be bad. We all know people who are buried in debt because of credit. Even credit cards can be good or bad. When we misuse them we could be drowning in debt. Some people never pay any interest on credit cards. They utilize the convenience, and even receive rewards for using them. The choice is theirs.

There is one credit that is always good, in fact, it is perfect. In Romans 4 the Word tells us, "Abraham believed God and it was credited to him for righteousness." Abraham was not righteous; he was like us, but because he believed (trusted), God proclaimed him righteous. When we believe and trust all that Jesus did at the cross, God gives each of us credit for being righteous. This is an everlasting glorious redemptive credit. Here is hoping that all who read this have or will have this very best of credit.

NEVER PASSES AWAY

None of the despots who ever lived or will live can ever destroy God's Word. Not Nero, Hitler, or anyone else can accomplish this.

God has always and will continue to keep his Word intact and He can certainly inform all His creation what He wants them to know and do. God said, "I don't have to write on tablets of stone (Moses' Law). I write on the fleshy part of everyone's heart." So all know the difference between right and wrong.

This world was framed by a Word. And this "Word" became flesh. Talk about power! God's Word, coupled with the Holy Spirit, produces "new birth." There is no scientific evidence, and no formula or equation that can explain the stabbing suddenness and thrilling power of God's Word! His Word is alive! We merely "share His Word in the power of the Holy Spirit," and leave the results to Him.

Again, this world that was framed by a Word is also influenced by a Word . . . even the words that we speak. Be careful . . . choose wisely . . . be kind to one another because we really don't know what kind of battle the other fellow is fighting.

Remember God's Words will never pass away and neither will ours!

BELIEVE IN YOUR HEART

The scripture says, "Believe in your heart and thou shalt be saved." (Romans 10:9)

Believing with your mind and believing with your heart are very different. You could believe because of all the press clippings and television news reports that a miraculous neurosurgeon was practicing in a large city. He could restore damaged skulls and brains. Let's say your little four year old son chased his ball into the street and was hit by a car that crushed his skull. You would move heaven and earth to make sure this great brain surgeon attended your son. When you laid his little crushed head onto the operating table, you would now believe not only with your mind, but with your heart. You put your best in his hands.

That is what we do when we believe in our hearts. We lay our very best, ourselves, on the line for the Great Physician. He works miracles in our hearts!

NEVER TOO OLD

Abraham was 75 when he responded to God's call. Caleb was 75 when he decided to do something more for the Lord. He is the inspiration for Caleb's Clans, Christian groups of older folks who still want to count for Jesus. They choose not to "get old and quit going" as against "if you quit going, you will get old."

Many of the world's greatest teachers and preachers were "past their so-called prime." God did not think so. He used them mightily!

Old folks saturated with the gospel can always find an empty table in the food court in the malls. Someone always comes by and asks if they can sit at your table. This provides an excellent opportunity to share. God has set up many "divine appointments" by this arrangement. A good old friend and part of our extended family trusted Jesus in his waning dying years. He was a fighter and doggedly hung onto life. Eventually, he slipped into a coma. Just before he drew his last breath, he rose slightly and said to his dear wife, "Honey, I am ready to go." My what a testimony! His same words were used at his funeral. They speak volumes even now. Would that all of us could say precisely the same, "Honey, I am ready to go." Remember:

We Are Never Too Old

GETTING PERSONAL

The speaker at one of our banquets, during a Weekend of Champions, is a dear friend of mine. Sometimes he gets rather personal with his comments.

On one occasion he said, "I'm not saying Cole (meaning me) is ugly, but when I looked up the word ugly in the dictionary, there was Cole's picture." Laughter ensued. He continued, "I'm not saying Cole is old, but when he went to high school, they didn't even have history." More laughter. Then he went too far and he started talking about my golf. He said, "Cole doesn't know it but he is on the back nine."

I immediately rose to my feet and very loudly announced, "My dear friend, you may be right about my being on the back nine, but what you don't understand is that I am playing thirty-six."

Some people get old and quit going. If we quit going we will get old. With God's help, I wish to keep going and doing what Jesus told Peter to do, "Feed my sheep."

A 25 YEAR OLD DRUNK

A 25 year old young man still living at home, had a terrible habit of getting drunk. One night he came home drunk about 3 am. The mother heard him go to his room. She waited patiently until she was sure he was asleep. She went into his room and saw the father of the young man, who had also heard his son come in. The daddy was rocking him back and forth in a rocking chair. He was also hugging him, and kissing his drunken son. The mother said, "Oh." The daddy said, "He won't let me love him when he is awake."

God wants to love all of us while we are awake!

WHAT'S ALL THIS FUSS ABOUT GIVING?
WHY GIVE?

* * * Giving is scriptural and spiritual.

* * * It gives us a sense of being honest with God.

* * * It makes us partners in the Great Commission.

* * * It enables us to be cheerful (hilarious) givers.

* * * Giving is one of the fulfilling things we will
        never regret!

* * * Best of all, it pleases Jesus!

God did not establish the principle of giving because He needed things. He merely knew we had to experience the joy of selfless giving.

We say, "The cattle on a thousand hills are the Lord's." "The earth is the Lord's and the fullness thereof." All this is very true, but the only money that the Lord has is what we are willing to give.

Jesus' last public official act with His little band was observing the treasury. This is the story of the widow's mite. Dear hearts, Jesus is still observing the treasury, yours and mine!

When we get to the end of the road, and we all are going to get there, let us not regret being less generous on the journey

"Count up your conquests on sea and land. Heap up your gold and hoard as you may. For all you can hold in your cold dead hand is what you have given away!" (Joaquin Miller).

Gifts we make today will impact someone's tomorrow, even their eternity.

"Although I appreciate your gifts, what makes me happy is the well-earned reward you will have because of your kindness."

Philippians 4:17 (Living Letters)

MONEY TALKS

Some people say money talks, and lots of money shouts. I never believed that money could talk. But one day I observed some money actually talking. There was a 100 dollar bill, a 20 dollar bill, and a 1 dollar bill. The 100 dollar bill was boasting about where he had been: big poker games, Vegas, Monte Carlo, and even in King's pockets. The 20 dollar bill said, " I have not been many places except the grocery store, the gas station, and a few other un-exciting places." The 1 dollar bill had to be coaxed to say anything. He finally said, "I haven't been anywhere except from church, to church, to church."

A RICH MANS WEALTH

A rich man tells this amazing story about his wealth. He said that making a lot of money was fun. He said managing the money was fun. But he said giving it away for God's causes is joy!

I CAN'T REMEMBER

An eleven-year-old girl from a small village in Brazil kept telling her parents that nearly every afternoon she would have a short meeting with Jesus. Her parents got the local priest involved. Even he believed her. They set up an audience with the Bishop. The Bishop asked the little girl if she was going to meet with Jesus the next day. The little girl assured him she would. The Bishop asked the child to ask Jesus about the last thing the Bishop confessed to Jesus. She agreed. At the meeting of the Bishop and the little girl the next day, the Bishop asked her, "Did you ask Jesus what was the last thing I confessed?" She said, "Yes, I did". The Bishop asked her "What did Jesus say?" She replied, "He said, 'I can't remember'."

"I'll remember your sins no more!"

THE PITS

It was Corrie Ten Boom who said that prisons are "the pits." She was absolutely correct. She also said, "There is no pit so deep that the love of Jesus is not deeper still."

There is a definite correlation between prisons and Hell. Jesus told of the bottomless pit, the abode of Hell. Prisons are terror. Hell is sheer terror! In prisons inmates regret the bad choices that caused their incarceration.

In Hell, a person is constantly haunted by his terror-filled conscious awareness of past stupidity and horrendous choices. One chooses Hell for oneself.

"The time came when the beggar died and the angels carried him to Abraham's side. The rich man also died and was buried. In hell, where he was in torment, he looked up and saw Abraham far away, with Lazarus by his side. So he called to him, "Father Abraham, have pity on me and send Lazarus to dip the tip of his finger in water and cool my tongue, because I am in agony in this fire.'

"But Abraham replied, "Son, remember that in your lifetime you received your good things, while Lazarus received bad things, but now he is comforted here and you are in agony. And besides all this, between us and you, a great chasm has been fixed, so that those who want to go from here to you cannot, nor can anyone cross over from there to us."

Luke 16: 22-26 NIV

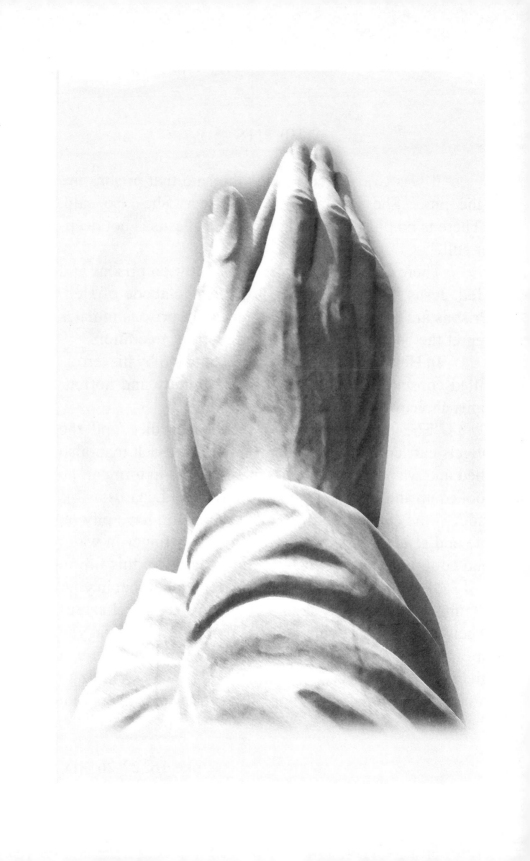

THE FERVENT PRAYER

God always answers prayers. His delay is not necessarily His denial. He always answers. In fact, when we pray, the answer is already on its way.

I had been a Christian only a few months when we received news that my Dad was in serious condition. He had a heart attack. He lived in Michigan and we lived in Kentucky. We rode the train all night. Betty and I prayed silently most of the trip. My prayer was very simple: "God, please spare my Dad from dying." Betty, who is much wiser, prayed, "Lord, please spare Bob's dad, so as to increase Bob's faith." Wow!

When we arrived at the hospital, as I was walking down the hall in the cardiac section, a tall man in a white coat asked me, "Are you the son of Ross Cole?" I answered, "Yes." He said, "Your dad is going to make it." Praise the Lord!

I remember what an old preacher said: "When you pray for rain, you should hear it thundering before you get off your knees." I do not claim to be "righteous" in the sense of super spiritual, so I can continue. I learned long ago that removing your halo will take a lot of weight off your mind.

"The effectual, fervent prayer of a righteous man availeth much." James 5:16 This truly says, "The winning, winning, winning, wins!" It is because of Him!

NO PATCHING

When God saves people, he doesn't just patch them up, He makes them brand new. There would not be enough patching in all the Goodyear plants to patch some of us.

Older folks know about patching for health problems! It's just patch, patch, patch.

The Lord says, "Therefore if any man be in Christ, he is a new creation."

So God makes us new, but He doesn't take away our personalities, our training, our gifts, and our experiences. He merely converts them. Paul, after the Damascus road encounter, retained his training, his knowledge of the Old Testament, and kept his Roman citizenship. These things were very helpful on his Christian journey.

When Christ first came into my life I knew I was "paid for," but I became a stupid prude. I burned all my cards, dice, and gambling paraphernalia. I wanted no part of all that. Later when my nine year old son Robert, joined a magic club, I was very upset. Magicians fooled with cards. Then, as a bolt of lightning out of the blue, I remembered Paul, the apostle. God did not take away Paul's gifts, He converted them! I decided to allow God to convert my abilities with cards. I made some magic tricks that I use in speaking engagements. The tricks entertain and establish the credentials for my story.

I also was taught early in the journey that conversion is not just an "about face," but a "to-the-rear march." It moves, it's alive, just as our Savior is alive! He's coming back soon! He's coming for the "new," not the "patched up"!
Praise The Lord!

FIRST DAY OF SPRING

The first day of spring and the first spring day are not necessarily one and the same. "Cold rain wintry," described the first day of spring this year. We still await the "first spring day." But why the weather report?

Spring and spring days are like some Christians. They may be "in season" but not "seasonable." They are "sayers" not "doers," especially in the area of stewardship and more specifically, tithing.

Christianity is not "I am because I do." Rather, "I do because I am." Tithing does not make me a Christian. But being a Christian makes me tithe.

A class of elderly Christian ladies puts us to shame when it comes to tithing and giving of love offerings. Pension monies, menial day labors, babysitting, house-keeping and other un-romantic jobs, of this 10% of all earnings and money received is the Lords."

They are taught this because the Bible teaches same. They believe and practice this grace because — (get this) they are Christian — Christ-Like — Of Christ! They are blessed for this giving and these love gifts. And my, aren't these dear ladies a blessing in themselves? You see, Jesus' sacrifice is meaningful and precious to them. They can do no less. The poem goes —

"Mary had a little lamb
What makes the lamb love Mary so?
Why, Mary loves the lamb, you know."

EASTER
(RESURRECTION OF TRUTH)

Seeing is believing, but meeting is more personal. Five times Jesus was seen and met on the first Easter. Easter is one of God's finest hours, and Jesus' suffering on the cross for hours makes it possible for a Christian's finest hour.

In Mark 16:9-15, we find "Meeting is believing." When we met Jesus and trusted Him as Lord and Savior, He got all of us. But my, my, my, we got all of Him! This is the bargain of Easter.

Since we have met Him, and since no one is born a Christian, and since God has no grandchildren, it is up to us to tell others about the Savior. We must introduce others to Him. They need to meet Him, too! Everyone deserves to hear the Gospel . . . eyeball to eyeball . . .heart to heart . . . soul to soul! God, the Holy Spirit will complete the introductions! Then they, too, can experience the joy of Easter.

"The Holy Scripture tells us that Jesus was seen five times on the resurrection day. He was seen of Mary; He was seen of the women; He was seen by two disciples on the road to Emmaus; He was seen by the apostles as they sat at meat. Later, he was seen by seven apostles by the sea, and by about five hundred at another time. He was seen by James and last of all, He was seen by Paul, earth's chiefest apostle. The evidences external and internal that Christ rose from the grave are overwhelming. That is our hope in the face of life; that is our hope in the face of death."

(George W. Truett)

NAKED

Corrie Ten Boom, in her book, "Hiding Place" has a great story.

It seems the concentration camp that held her and her sister had some hideous guards. One day they lined up a hundred of the women in single file. The guards then demanded the women take off all their clothes. They complied under the leering lecherous eyes of their captors. This was a terrible, humiliating, debasing ordeal. Then Corrie remembered her Savior on the Cross! She leaned over to her sister and said, "Take heart, they took all His clothes off, too."

"By His Stripes We Are Healed"

NO OPTIONS

When we told God we were sorry for our sins, and invited Jesus into our hearts, He made us "brand new." New everything, but He let us keep our own personalities and our choices. We gave up certain options. Judging is one of the foremost. (This is God's business.) We gave up lying and stealing and adultery and coveting and so on. We also gave up gossiping. (A nasty, debilitating habit.) We gave up these options.

Another major area is to witness or not to witness. We gave up the option not to witness.

We gave up the option not to reach people, and we kept the option to reach people. Reaching persons:

"Reaching persons for Christ and His church is not a dated emphasis but a continuing task; not the responsibility of special groups, but of every disciple; not limited to special seasons but for every day; not for an interim but for the age. It is not a tributary but the main stream of God's concern for all people."

Author Unknown

It has been said, "The Gospel is all important or not important. What it cannot be is moderately important." We choose to believe it is all important. So is reaching persons.

"We Retain The Option Of Joy In The Lord"

HOME GROWN SAYINGS

- Home is where life makes up its mind about everything that matters.
- Difficulty is one excuse the Lord will not accept.
- Give out, but don't give up.
- Attitude is the grit to grapple with life.
- Why not go out on a limb? Isn't that where the fruit is?
- Heartbeats are numbered. What are you spending them on?
- Ignorance of the Bible means ignorance of Jesus!
- There is nothing more pitiful than a half-filled Christian trying to overflow.
- Jesus is enough!
- Bumper Stickers:
  * God Loves You Anyway
  * Look Busy, Jesus is Coming
  * Life is Short — Pray Hard
- Character (essence of one's being)
  1. Character is always shown by the choices we make.
  2. Character is always tested by what it takes to stop us.
  3. Character is doing right even when no one is looking.
- Best heart exercise is reaching down and helping someone up.
- We can never get anyone to do better by telling them how bad they are.
- The accent of love will penetrate where the tones of anger could never find a way!

God Is Love!
And
God So Loved!

WINSOME

Paul said, "I am all things to all men that I might win some." He was truly "winsome" as he won some. He was so winsome that they listened to him all night, and they would fall out of the balcony and be revived and listen again all day. He was probably the second most winsome of all, Jesus being first and foremost.

I firmly believe that it is incumbent upon all of us to be winsome. The scripture says we should be full of grace. Many of our preacher evangelists are wonderfully winsome. For instance, Billy Graham, Billy Sunday, Bill Glass, and Bill Bright. This makes you wish your name was "Bill." The point of all this is that all of the above are winsome, winsome, winsome!

ATTITUDE

'THE GRIT TO GRAPPLE WITH LIFE"

Sometimes we need some help with our attitudes — maybe an adjustment. One sure help is when we make ourselves remember when we first met Jesus. This was a time of real freedom and relief and a time of uncluttered love and emotions. It was a time where gratitude grew and welled up into unfeigned love. That is when we knew that we loved Jesus more than anything, and that HE loved us best of all. And we wanted everyone to feel the same. It was a time when our blessings were too many to count. This was real contentment, and we knew God was on His throne, and all was well with our souls.

"Contentment makes poor men rich, and conversely."

Ben Franklin

CHOICE OF ATTITUDE

Rev. Caudill served a small Baptist church in Cuba. Then Castro took over and things changed. He was told to stop preaching. He would not, so they arrested him and put him into jail. Caudill thought he would be like the Apostle Paul, and so he preached to his jailers. Then they put him in "the hole," a dungeon-like place with only a couple of rats for companions. After a few weeks he became very bitter about his circumstances.

He was lying on the floor of his damp cell one night. He was half asleep and still grumbling. Then in semi-consciousness he heard God's voice saying, "You don't have anything. Everyone has deserted you. You really don't have anything, do you?" Caudill answered, "You know I don't have anything." God repeated the question. Caudill answered the same. God said, "Wrong, Caudill, you still have a choice of your attitude." Caudill pondered for a moment and said, "You are right, Lord, and I am sorry for my bad attitude."

Caudill began remembering the wonder and beauty of God's promises. His attitude changed. One week later he was released and sent back to the States. This story became the basis of a very long and successful preaching career.

God Is Faithful!

SELF ESTEEM

Self esteem, self worth, self image, these three mean the same. A good definition for self esteem is "pride in being a human being."

Everything any of us does, whether positive or negative, stems from our own self esteem. This poor or low self esteem is a common denominator among inmates. The very fact that they are locked up inside and the rest of us are on the outside, says volumes. No wonder they call people on the outside, "people of the free world." Once a person's freedom is taken away from them, they are hurting, especially their self esteem.

There is only one cure for poor self esteem. His name is Jesus.

*"You shall know the truth,
and the truth shall make you free."*

John 8:32

ZACCHAEUS (LOW SELF ESTEEM)

When we first meet Zacchaeus, we find a man with low self-esteem. He thought he needed to make people notice him, so he took a job as a Roman tax collector. This was not good for his self-esteem. His own people, the Jews, hated him, and so did the Romans. He felt like he was on the lowest rung of life's ladder. He desperately needed help.

He heard about this miracle worker, Jesus, who was visiting his town. He really needed to see Him. He scrambled up a sycamore tree near the road Jesus was travelling. He climbed out onto a big fat limb for a good vantage-point. At least, he could get a glimpse of Jesus. Jesus did a very strange thing. He crossed the road and walked under the sycamore tree, and looked up at Zacchaeus. Zacchaeus' heart began pounding, and he said to himself, "He sees me, He sees me!" Jesus sees all of us all of the time. Then Jesus did another startling thing. He said, "Zacchaeus!" Now Zacchaeus' blood pressure rose dramatically, along with his racing heart. Zacchaeus said, "He knows me, He knows me!" Christ knows all of us, even before our birth. Zacchaeus also saw himself for the first time, and he was not pleased. He wanted to be like Jesus.

Then our Lord gave Zacchaeus a surprising invitation. He said, "Zacchaeus, come down. I want to go with you to your home." At this point, Zacchaeus' blood pressure is off the chart and his heart is speeding. Zacchaeus said to himself, "He wants me, He wants me!" Jesus wants everyone. Then in Zacchaeus' "heart of hearts," where he gets his stuff together, Zacchaeus said, "He can have me, He can have me!" This was a brilliant response for Zacchaeus and for everyone.

He restored Zacchaeus along with his self-image. He truly is a "miracle-working God."

FATHER IMAGE

(GOD GIVEN)

"Home is where life makes up its mind about everything that matters." A God-given father image is crucial for the family. This father image reflects our Heavenly Father, and is highly important to the children.

A close examination of the Kennedy killers reveals a lot pertaining to the lack of a God-given father image. Lee Harvey Oswald's father was totally absent during Lee's formative years. Sirhan Sirhan's father was in Lebanon during Sirhan's formative years. Both killers were devoid of a good father image.

Dr. Ralph Gabler and Len O'Connor, a newspaper analyst from Chicago, made some startling discoveries when they interviewed 1160 inmates in Joliet State Prison. They found that nearly all the inmates had bad fathers. Their dads drank, didn't provide, beat their mothers, and some fathers were unknown and almost non-existent. Most of the inmates said of their fathers that they couldn't talk to them.

It is highly desirable to keep the lines of communication open between a father and his children. As the father pulls away from the child, the child pulls away from the father. This distance gets squared in a hurry.

Remember, "The accent of love will penetrate where the tones of anger could never find a way."

God's norm remains: One Man, One Woman, One Family for Life!

CORRECT WORDS

Noah Webster was a stickler for using correct words. After all, he was probably the world's greatest lexicographer.

Noah was a little flirtatious. One day his wife was descending their long staircase. Near the bottom of the steps she saw Noah kissing the French maid on the back of her neck. Noah's wife exclaimed, "Noah, I am surprised!" Noah said, "No, no my dear, you are astounded, I am surprised."

Correct words are vital. Battles have been won or lost, quarrels have ensued, and marriages have been dissolved because of what was said.

We must be careful what we say and how we say it. Remember, the accent of love will penetrate where the tones of anger could never find a way.

We communicate in various ways, across many vehicles, like wires, beams, internet etc.

Always remember – The very best vehicle we can communicate across is love!

Love is never satisfied by any response but love.

God Is Love!

"Pleasant words are as an honeycomb, sweet to the soul, and health to the bones."

Proverbs 16:24

PUNGENT ACTIVITY VERBS
PREGNANT WITH MEANING

When Jesus tells us to do something, He uses pungent activity verbs. The list contains *love, go, do share, teach, tell, help, make, witness* and so on. It is like the King of Kings, the Lord of Lords, and the General of the Universe saying to us buck privates, "Get with it!" This is a direct command! "Get with it!" while it is day. When we do, we will hear the most precious words of all eternities. These will be words of approval, affirmation, appreciation, and acceptance. They will be spoken by the Lord Jesus Himself, who has our un-dying adoration!

"Well Done Thy Good
And Faithful Servant!"

FAITH CAME SINGING

Faith came singing into my room

And other Guests took flight.

Fear and Gloom, and Dread and Doom

Sped out into the night.

I wondered and pondered

how that could be

But Faith said gently,

"Can't you see

They could never, ever

Live with me."

Bob Cole 1974

FAITH (A GAMBLE?)

The writer of Hebrews says, "Without faith it is impossible to please God." This is a powerful soul-searching statement.

It appears that it takes a lot more faith not to believe the biblical account of God's redemptive plan, than it takes faith to believe. Creation itself is more than ample proof. Even Einstein made a profound statement of faith after he gazed into the heavens through the telescope at Mount Palomar. He said, "There must be a divine architect."

Let us say that Christianity is a hoax, and that saving faith is a gamble at best. In Christianity, you merely put up faith in God and what Christ did for us at Calvary and the result is that we gain the whole world, so to speak. But, if we gamble that our puny thoughts and ideas are superior, then we put up all we have or ever hope to have and gain perdition for our efforts. We are not only betting our lives, but we are betting our eternities, too! We can't afford to lose this bet.

Dr. Jack McGorman, an outstanding teacher, preacher, and author from Southwestern Seminary, is a dear, precious friend. Dr. McGorman confided in me that his son, Stephen, was dying of cancer. Stephen was in the hospital isolation area for a bone marrow transplant. Stephen, a very learned man, was a non-believer. The dear professor was heartbroken. Dr. McGorman had an appointment to see Stephen in the hospital the next evening. We prayed about the meeting. I suggested to my dear friend to say right off to his son, "I am your Father, and only Pastor, and I have ample reason to share something with you." I then asked Dr. McGorman to tell Stephen about the "Gamble Story." Tell him that an ex-hoodlum suggested this.

Dr. McGorman told me a couple of days later about his visit. He said that Stephen seemed to take this story at face value. Stephen said, "I remember my elderly Sunday School teacher telling me something very similar." Stephen died soon after. We are not privy to what transpired between God and Stephen. We only know that God is merciful, long-suffering and faithful. We know God answers prayers. It only takes a moment to become a Christian.

Incidentally, if faith or Christianity is a gamble, it's the only one we are going to have. Your author and countless millions of others can attest that faith in God is a sure thing! You can bet your life and your eternity! "For God so loved the world . . ."

WISDOM PERSONIFIED

"If anyone lacks wisdom let him ask God and it shall be given unto him." After we have searched the scriptures for wisdom, then we need to seek out godly counselors.

Today, as I talked on the phone with my dear friend, Dr. Jack McGorman, I felt I was in the presence of greatness. I had a similar experience while playing golf with Billy Graham. These blessed encounters will forever be etched in my memory bank.

Dr. McGorman and I relived some of the wonders of God's grace, as the power of the Holy Spirit moved upon all of us in the prisons. We jogged each other's memories of these Holy Spirit power laden occasions. My dear professor friend did most of the talking. It was much better that way.

I told my dear friend about *"Gems for the Journey"*, and more specifically the story pertaining to his son, Stephen. Our memories matched. Dr. McGorman said he was pleased with the story about his son. He verified the entire episode. He also encouraged me about the *"Gems"*. He said he was pleased with the title of the book, and then went on to explain. I drank it all in! Here again, when one is in the Presence of Wisdom, Listen!

We considered the possibility of getting copies of *"Gems for the Journey"* into the hands of graduating seminarians. God will provide.

We talked for about forty minutes. It seemed much shorter. I did not want to end the conversation. As we reluctantly said our "goodbyes", we agreed to stay in touch. We also encouraged each other to "keep on, keeping on".

Many writers seem to infer that Wisdom is a lady. Wisdom can also be a gentleman. I talked with Wisdom today!

If I should live to a ripe old age

may I possess some bit of

individuality, charm and wit,

that I may not be discarded

when I am withered, worn and

weak, but sought after and

cherished like a fine antique.

Author Unknown

PLANNED VERSUS CANNED

Since sharing Christ is the most important pre-requisite we have, we should be as efficient and professional as possible. We need to practice our speeches in front of a mirror: gestures, pauses, volume, and all. We need to get it down "pat."

Some say, "Isn't that pretty much canned?" No – No – No! "It is not canned, it is planned." Planned is much better. God has wonderful plans for us.

> "For I know the plans I have for you,
> says the Lord, they are plans for good
> and not for evil, to give you a future
> and a hope."

Jeremiah 29: II Living Letters

THREE P'S

PRIDE – False view of oneself.

PREJUDICE – False view of others.

PRESUMPTION – False view of God.

The last "P" puts one in a precarious position. A drastic change is needed to avoid reaping for oneself sheer terror!

AGAPE

Agape is God's Love. This Greek word for love is what Jesus used when he asked Peter, "Do you love me?" Peter answered all three times with another Greek word for love, "Phileo." It satisfied Jesus.

We can only scratch the surface of the full meaning of Agape.

* Unconditional
* Willful
* Intelligent
* Commitment
(Dr. Robert McMillan)

Agape also means, "I will become what is necessary to help you become." During a "Champions for Life" weekend, I become an inmate, so in turn the inmate might become a child of God. We know for a fact that Jesus was the miracle of becoming what we are, so that we, in turn, could start becoming like Him.

Agape is tied into the verb, "to be." "Hid with Christ in God". "Christ in you the only hope of glory." "I and the Father are one." Our finite minds cannot grasp it all except to say,

Jesus Loves Me!
This I Know!

OUR THEME SONG

*So, everywhere we go, we talk
about Christ to all who will listen,
warning them and teaching them,
as well as we know how. We want to
be able to present each one to God,
perfect, because of what Christ has
done for each of them.
This is my work and I can do it
only because Christ's mighty
energy is at work within me.*

Colossians 1:28, 29
Living Bible

DOUBLE TOUGH

Colossians 3:17 and 3:23 are very similar, or so it seems at first reading.

Colossians 3:17 "And whatsoever ye do in word or deed, do in the name of the Lord Jesus." The gist of this verse is that we minister as though we were Jesus.

Colossians 3:23 "And whatsoever ye do, do it heartily as to the Lord" – The "warp and woof" and the clearest meaning here is that we are to minister as though we are ministering unto Jesus himself. Mother Theresa's people were taught this.

Verse 17 says we minister as though we are Jesus. Verse 23 says we minister as though we are ministering unto Jesus. This is DOUBLE TOUGH. But it is not too tough for the people who go with us in the prisons. It is fairly easy for them and very natural. "It's as natural as a goose going barefoot." I believe they call this "lifestyle evangelism." It's really not –

Double Tough

DISCIPLE
LEARNER-FOLLOWER

We can state the definition either way: a learner who is following or a follower who is learning. When Jesus said, "Take my yoke upon me and learn of me," He was in deadly earnest. On occasion, He chided His disciples for slow learning. So it is imperative that we learn of Him! Ignorance of the Bible means ignorance of Jesus.

Lincoln said, "I don't think much of a person who doesn't know more today than he did yesterday." Our friend Tremendous Jones says, "But for the books you read and the people you meet, you'll be the same person five years from now as you are today." We need to learn, "while it is day", or is it really almost midnight?

Someone said, "One thing certain that we learn from history, is that we don't learn from history." In our studies of great civilizations of the past that went down the drain, we can deduce a couple of problems that were devastating. The "fall" part of *The Rise And Fall of the Roman Empire* exposes these two glaring faults. They are:

1. The breakdown of the family unit.
2. The unnatural attraction and the misuse of the human body.

These two obvious defects are now part and parcel of our culture!

These facts should urgently prompt all of us to action. We who are followers need to learn and apply our learning. When we do, people will note "that we have been with Jesus."

Learners continue to follow and followers continue to learn! Jesus never said it was going to be easy; He said He would be with us!

"Trying to absorb the depths
of the Bible is like
trying to mop up the
ocean floor with a sponge."

Anonymous

WHAT IS NUMBER ONE?

Some years ago, I was invited to lead in a soul-winning conference in a rather large church in Orlando, Florida. The audience consisted of about 50 pastors and about 250 deacons. The fellowship hall was used for the meeting. The seating was arranged in a semi-circle with about 10 rows of participants. I sat in a swivel chair in front of the audience. The blackboard was behind me.

After the greeting, I asked a very soul-searching question. I asked the audience to tell me; "What did God have in mind for us to do? Why were we put here on earth? How come He chose us? What is our top priority? What is the total aggrandizement of what we're about?" There was a deadly silence for about 30 seconds. This is a long time in a room full of people. Finally, a deacon rose to his feet and said, "Win the world for Christ." The audience started springing up like wheat. The bulk of their answers were very similar to the first. Then the responses subsided.

I told them in loving terms their responses were great and wonderful, but wrong! I explained that Jesus was asked a very similar question and His answer was much different. He said, "Love the Lord your God with all your heart, mind, soul, and strength." He went on to say, "Love your neighbor as you love yourself." They are in this order:

1. Love God (foremost)
2. Love Yourself
3. Love your neighbor

When we get number one right, the others fall in place. We cannot love our neighbor without first loving ourselves.

God did not make any junk when He made us! God does not book any flops! We are His highest creation! We are all made in God's image. (Note the plurality)

I am not saying we should be pompous idiots, or braggadocios ego-maniacs. I am saying that we are eternal and God wants to fellowship with us in love.

He Proved This At Calvary!

NAMELESS PEOPLE

How many scholars are there among us who can tell the names of those shepherds who received the great announcement of the birth of Jesus? Who among us knows the name of the woman at the well? Can any of us recite the name of the fellow who was carrying a water pot on his head? Jesus said, "Follow him, he has my room set up [for the Lord's Supper]." We do not know any of these persons names. This plainly says that God uses nameless people like you and me for His eternal purposes!

We truly are the right persons, at the right time, and the right place, with the right message!

LAST BEST HOPE

America and the whole world is in crisis. The 9 11 tragedy contributed to this. It is as though God is saying to us, "You had better get serious about Me."

In another crisis for America, President Lincoln said, "We are man's last best hope." Borrowing from President Lincoln we can say, "We who name the name of Christ, are God's last best hope. We shall either meanly lose or nobly save God's last best hope!"

There is a series of axioms that say:

What we don't know, we can't define or talk about.
What we can't talk about, we can't use.
What we can't use, we can't save!

This is definitely appropriate to sharing the gospel. We shall either meanly lose, like sniveling cowards, or nobly save, like children of the King,

God's Last Best Hope!

"I WILL RETURN"

Many years before General McArthur said, "I shall return," our Lord said precisely the same. Christ's return is a popular recurrent theme of the New Testament writers. The Bible is crowded with the grand news of Jesus' second coming.

And so it is, our Father, in whoever's company we stand, we think of the precious moment when we shall soar to the Heavens with our Savior. But until that precious moment, may our waking hours and even our dreams reveal the message of Jesus that surges from our very being.

We concur most heartily with the final prayer of the scriptures, "Even so come quickly, Lord Jesus."

IT'S LATE

A very old couple were sleeping in one morning. Their chime clock started bonging and bonging, and would not stop. Finally, the old lady said, "John, John, get up, it is later than it ever has been." She was absolutely correct, it is later than it's ever been.

Some of our airmen were captured in the Vietnam war. When they were released from their prisons in Hanoi, each prisoner of war said practically the same thing. Whether they had been in prison only a few months or even for years, they all made this startling revelation. They were all shocked by how our country was sliding into a disastrous moral decline. The rest of us seemed to be under a form of Chinese water torture, only one drop at a time. We did not seem to be aware of the slide.

Our servicemen were shocked and embarrassed. We should be! Nearly all the news and entertainment industry has sold out to the Devil and his crowd. Jesus did tell us that "times would wax worse and worse."

It is time to re-examine that bumper sticker which reads:

"Get Busy, Jesus Is Coming!"

TRUTH

"Ye shall know the truth and the truth shall set you free." Truth and freedom are compatible. Franklin Delano Roosevelt said, "The truth is found when men are free to pursue it."

Pilate asked Jesus in John's Gospel, "What then is truth?" Jesus, the perfect truth, did not answer him. Truth needs no defense. It just stands there and remains the truth.

I tell inmates on occasion, "Let's say that wall is the truth. Run into it and you will bounce back. The truth just stands there. Jesus is the truth! The Word says very plainly, "Ye shall know the truth and the truth shall set you free. If the Son shall set you free, ye shall be free indeed."

Freedom is the hope and dream of every prisoner. Everyone without Christ is a prisoner, of his own ego and this cosmos (world). Jesus said it best, "Ye are of your father the devil."

We all need to be free! Jesus is the doorway to Freedom. When you are free, it doesn't make any difference what happens, because you are paid for. You can soar to the Heavens like a bird. You are free! You have embraced the Truth.

CUSTER'S LAST WORDS
(This is certainly not a so-tale)

Once upon a time, I spoke to a fairly large group of men. I made the comment: "I needed that about like General Custer needed some more Navajos." Shortly after the speech, a young native Indian asked if he could speak frankly. I said, "Sure, why not?" He said, "Mr. Cole, you really don't know a whole lot about American history, especially about the Battle of the Little Bighorn." I agreed. He continued to tell me that his great grandfather was a chief and was involved in that battle. He says there were no Navajos, just Sioux and Cheyenne. He also said that there is a lot of misconception about what Custer said. He did not say, "Where in the world did all these Indians come from?" He also did not say, "Men take no prisoners." But Grandfather did overhear Custer say, "Why didn't you fellows act this way at the dance last night?" Grandfather said he also heard Custer's last word. It was "ugh". . . right after a spear had found its mark.

(I warned you that this was not a "so-tale")

VERY ODD DEFINITIONS

* *Rich*   Enough money to burn a wet donkey

* *Grouch*   Someone who owns and operates an acid
             disposition

* *Fanatic* Someone who has lost sight of his goal and
             redoubled his efforts

* *Cheap*   Closer than the paper on the wall
             Closer than a dead heat
             Closer than 19 to 20

* *Can't get his stuff together* means, "He's dropped his stick."

* *"An intellectual* is someone who is educated beyond his
   intelligence" Rep. Henry Hyde

HOME-GROWN DEFINITIONS

• Integrity means, "I will do what I say I'll do."

• Attitude means "the grit to grapple with life."
  (In most cases attitude surpasses aptitude.)

• Character (Essence of one's being) It means doing right
  on purpose, even when no one is watching.

• Character is always shown by the choices one makes.

• Character is always tested, by what it takes to stop us
  from being the people we should be. Only God can
  give us a brand-new character.

• Contentment makes poor men rich and conversely.

• Empathy means "Sympathy on a two-way street."
  "I want to share with you the same way that I would like
  you to share with me." "I'll change seats with you."

• The eleventh commandment is, "Be flexible; don't
  get bent out of shape."

• Enthusiasm is confidence and knowledge shared.
  It's free.

2 – NUMBER SERMON

The next day after Jesus came into my heart with a thrilling, exciting Holy Intrusion (This is how I was saved), my father-in-law visited me in the showroom where I sold cars. He said, "You know I'm not a preacher, but one day in every seven belong to The Lord, and one dime of every dollar you earn belongs to Him." These are the (2) numbers.

I told him, "I got it!"

"Count up your conquests of sea and land, heap up your gold, and hoard as you may. For all you can hold in your cold dead hand is what you have given away."

(Joaquin Miller)

Who wants to be the richest guy in the graveyard?

A good Philosophy of Life:

In order to get everything I want out of life, I've got to make sure you're getting what you want out of life.

I'm going to sell you this car the same way I would want you to sell it to me.

These are takeoffs on the golden rule, truly the superior philosophy.

PRIORITIES

Sometimes when our priorities get out of whack, we start "spinning like a barber pole." We really can't get our "stuff" together. God knew this and He gave us a list of priorities.

In the Garden experience, He laid them out. We are welcome to argue with this list, but we will be arguing with God. Here is the order:

1. Jesus (Savior, God) First & Foremost
2. Mate (not family, just your mate)
3. Children (equally important)
4. Job (what we do to earn a living)
5. Church and related ministry

The Bible is loaded with accounts where even the saints of God got their priorities out of order and trouble ensued.

A Sunday School superintendent served many years in a large church. His wife of 20 years left him. She played "second fiddle" to his church job. He put priority number 5 in front of number 2. It was very costly and unnecessary.

We probably need to spend more time in Genesis. Ignorance of the Bible is ignorance of Jesus. May God "open the eyes of our hearts!"

MARY HAD A LITTLE LAMB

This is a very familiar little poem and with no intention of doing this beautiful poem any harm, we could also say it thusly:

Mary had a little lamb,
Its fleece was white as snow.
And everywhere that Mary went
The lamb was sure to go.
What makes the lamb love Mary so?
Why Mary loves the lamb you know.

David honored God. God honored David. We love God because He first loved us. Sharing this "Good News" love should be one of our top priorities to give folks hope. "The single greatest need facing the human race today, our very survival as a species depends on hope, and without hope, we will lose the faith that we can cope."

Hope in the scriptures usually means confident expectation and assurance, and a guarantee of something wonderful. "Christ in you the only hope of glory." God's promises are sure and solid. He keeps His Word!

NOT MUCH TO GIVE

"Christmas has really caught us at a bad time. We've bought out. Our money has disappeared. Just can't give any more. We have been nickled and dimed to death."

BUT –

Doesn't cost much to smile.
        A friend might need cheering up.
Doesn't cost much to sincerely say,
        "How are you feeling?"
Doesn't cost much to visit a sick friend,
        or anyone for that matter.
Doesn't cost much to listen,
        to lend a sympathetic ear.
Doesn't cost much to witness to a lost person.

You can't guarantee him hope, but you can
        introduce him to your Savior Friend, who can.
You can't save him, but your Friend can.
You can't give him eternal security, but your Friend can.

        Really has been a hard dry season; not much to give!

December 1964

WHAT IS CHRISTMAS?

You say it is children's laughter, gifts, toys, sugar-plums; or grown-ups' gifts, toys, revelry, gaiety, vacation.

These few words might shed some light on its meaning: bristling, befitting, bewildering, beautifying, binding, ballyhooing, bewitching, bustling; or maybe, busy buyers in bargain basements begetting better buys; or BEING BORN – BIRTH OF A BABY IN BETHLE-HEM'S BARN!

Why that's it! That's Christmas – God's Gift. All of the other things were gifts, but this is God's Gift. Here is the greatest most precious Gift of all ages – the BABY OF BETHLEHEM'S BARN – JESUS!

The Bible says: unspeakable Gift, unsearchable riches; yet words cannot illumine this gracious, generous, Godly Gift.

In this season, we have an opportunity to present a gift to our Jesus on His Birthday.

It has been said, "You can give without loving, but you cannot love without giving!"

Christmas 1963

MAGIC OF CHRISTMAS

* Many things are wrong with our culture, but Christmas is not one of them.

* Christmas is too large to be stuffed into a little child's stocking.

* Having Christmas in your heart puts Christmas in the air.

* A time for giving, not swapping.

* Surely the hinge of history was on Bethlehem's barn.

* Learn to take Christmas one day at a time, all year long.

GOD'S CHRISTMAS GIFT

"God so loved the world that He gave His one and only Son, that whoever believes in Him shall not perish but have eternal life" (John 3:16, NIV).

Love is never satisfied by any response but love!

*T*was the day after Christmas

and all thru the house

All the creatures were stirring,

The Kids, Mate and the Spouse.

All thankful and grateful

for gifts of such pleasure

And sweet memories for all

that each could so treasure.

but the greatest of thoughts

that to each one of us clings,

Is that Jesus Is Ours —

The best Gift that God brings.

Bob Cole
Christmas 1982

BASEBALL CHAPEL

Major league baseball players are plying their trade on Sundays. They have no opportunity to go to church, so "church" comes to them. Over forty years ago, Waddy Spoelstra and some others came up with the idea of having chapel services at major league stadiums. Sometimes the programs are in the locker room or in a room close by. Each program features a guest who speaks for about twenty minutes. A chapel leader, usually a ball player, invites the speakers. These programs are well-attended. God blesses in a powerful way and many young men make life-changing commitments.

I recall one occasion when the Giants were playing the Big Red Machine in Cincinnati. It was raining and neither team could take infield practice so we had ample time to present the Gospel. The Holy Spirit took charge of the meeting and many players trusted Christ. The fellowship was so great that the manager had to ask his team over and over to go play ball! The Lord can make us impervious to mundane things. Our dear departed friend, Waddy, is sitting on the celestial curbstone still admiring Baseball Chapel, and so is God!

Over the last thirty years, I have met again a number of these major league baseball stars. Many have recounted our first meeting when they prayed to receive Christ. This says, "The laborer is worthy of his hire."

THREE STRIKES – YOU'RE OUT!

"Three strikes, you're out!" is part and parcel of baseball. A major league umpire gave his explanation about pitches. He said, "Some are balls and some are strikes, but they ain't nothin 'til I call 'em." This is simple but profound.

The Supreme Umpire of the universe calls every pitch correctly. He doesn't abide by the rule that says, "Three strikes – you're out!" If He did, then all the heroes of faith in Hebrew 11 would have been called out early in the game. Most of us would be in that group. He gives us a whole bunch of strikes. Praise His Name!

Abraham kept missing the ball when he was a hundred years old. Sarah was ninety and "couldn't hit the side of a barn." Paul the apostle had untold strikes on him. Our ability to hit doesn't amount to much. It was Jesus who hit the home run with the bases loaded at Calvary.

This is not to say we should not continue to take our turn at bat. Stay in the game. Step up to the plate. Don't bail out. And never, never give up. Give out, but don't give up. Yogi was right, "It's not over 'til it's over". Give it your best shot and keep swinging until you hear,

"Well Done Thy Good
And Faithful Servant"

CHRISTIAN GOLFER

God even allows Christians to play golf, as long as it doesn't interfere with higher priorities.

On one occasion a Christian golfer was matched up with another player. Neither could really play that well. The player other than the Christian started using the Lord's name in vain after every bad shot, and that was very often. Finally, each time that he used the Lord's name in anger, the Christian would answer, "Praise the Lord." After a few times of this routine, the golfer said, "How come you always say that after I say something?" The Christian answered, "I only want to give God equal time." The cursing subsided. In a little while the weather was looking ominous. There was lightning in the distance. The one golfer said to the Christian, "Can't you do something about this weather?" The Christian answered, "NO, I am in sales, not service."

All who name the name of Christ are in "sales." Good, bad, or indifferent, we are still in "sales"!

ONE BALL – ONE LIFE

Some years ago, a very memorable event took place in a golf match. John and I were partners in a two ball match play with a real character, named Brubaker, and his friend Bill.

My partner's ball came to rest about a foot from the hole. I was tending the flag for my partner's putt. I inadvertently knocked my partner's ball back to him and said, "It's good." This precipitated a whirlwind of a one-sided ruckus.

Brubaker who was one of my opponents went berserk! Now Brubaker weighs about 130 lbs. soaking wet. I weigh twice that much. Size did not deter Brubaker. He rushed up to me and pointed his finger at me until he actually touched my nose. He said over and over very loudly, "You are responsible for one ball!" I can still hear him saying that. Everybody within a mile of us could hear it also.

What he said was very amusing yet extremely profound. We are all responsible for only one ball – one life.

Certainly we are to be concerned and caring for others, but our ultimate responsibility is for ourselves and our God.

Incidentally, the only person we can be certain of improving is ourselves. Our choices reflect our responsibilities. Our choices determine our love and devotion to God, to our mates, our children and so on.

All of us have only one "ball" – "life" to make choices for. We need to be careful about those choices.

"Choose This Day Whom You Will Serve"

GOD GIVEN LIFE THEMES

God, who is the author and giver of all life, is also the giver of life themes. These following themes are very prominent in successful sales persons. They are crucial for the gospel's sake.

This great democracy of ours flourishes and thrives on selling. If there were no sales people manufacturing would soon be extinct. "Nothing happens until somebody sells something." This statement is etched in stone. It is a veritable truism! In a free society selling is the catalyst for industry. It is vital!

An accomplished sales person has learned well the following:

1. We don't make people buy anything!
   We merely make them want to.
2. The sale is always made in the buyer's mind.
3. We must sell with the buyer's benefits in mind.

These three pertinent approaches to selling separate the winners from the also rans.

The following are some God Given Life Themes. These are part and parcel to winning leaders and sales people. "Leaders are dealers in hope". Napoleon Bonaparte

A. Courage is primary. Winston Churchill said,
   "Courage is first of Human qualities because
   it is the quality which guarantees all the others."
   Courage is the quality of becoming more

determined in the face of resistance i.e. obstacles.
Courage breeds stick-to-it-ive-ness. Courage
is the Father of persistency. Babies demonstrate
this life theme when they attempt to crawl,
stand, and walk. They fall often, but they
don't give up.

B. Ego-drive is the desire to be recognized as a
significant person and a craving for self-
esteem (pride in being a human being).
Realize, "God does not make any junk."
We are all unique, one of a kind. We are
a million times a million different from
anyone else. God did not make a mistake
when He made us. He says we are highly
important to Him. He says we are special –
because we are!

It is how we handle the "pats on the back and
awards" that show our dependence on Him and
shows our thankfulness to Him.

C. Affirmation: Drive. We want to be accepted
and liked by others.

D. Communication skills
    1. Fluency is the use of words that are positive.
    2. Zest is the art of gaining and holding
       attention by a unique and appealing use

of words. Zest is the more important of
the two.

E. Relator – A "Good Mixer" with the knack of
   establishing quick and easy and friendly
   relationships. Relators are sensitive to the
   needs and wants of others, and they signal
   their desire to be of service.

F. Integrity means, "I will do what I say I will
   do." This theme will guarantee repeat
   business and many referrals.

There are many more traits or life themes in successful sales persons but these are crucial. These traits are
loaded with some attributes of Christ Himself and they
most assuredly embody the Golden Rule, "Do unto others
as you would have them do unto you." "I am going to sell
you this product the same way I would want you to sell it
to me." God's way is superior!

Psalm 84:11 "No good thing will He withhold from them
who walk uprightly".

SALIENT TRUTHS

*If we leave Jesus undiscovered, we will leave life's vital issues unattended. (The most vital issue is eternity.)

* Since our God whom we know and love and serve, goes to the funeral of a sparrow, we can bet our bottom dollar that He will hear anyone that cries out to Him!

* When our situation is the bleakest – when we are sure our boat is going to sink – when we have heard some horrible news that has shrunk our priorities: Even in our darkest hour, God always breaks thru with His brightest hope, Jesus!

* David and Israel had numerous battles with the Philistines. On one occasion, just before a battle, David prayed and sought God's face. God answered. He told David to make a frontal assault and the battle would be won! David did just that, and Victory! At another time just before the battle with the same enemy, David prayed and sought God's face. This time God told David, "Wait till you hear my army marching through the tree tops, then you fight a rear guard action and the battle shall be yours". (Whoever heard of an army marching through the trees!) David did just as God said. He fought a rear guard action and won! The scripture said on that occasion, "God is the God of the breakthrough." He was then and He is now!

The God Of The Breakthrough!

PROOFS FOR THE WORD
(AN OXYMORON FOR A TITLE)

Some years ago, in some long-hidden caves in the Holy Land, the Dead Seas Scrolls were found. They revealed and were almost verbatim to some Old Testament scriptures. This "find" did not prove the Bible, it merely proved they dug in the right place. The Bible is always Truth!

Many so-called scholars of scripture believed that our first gospel writer, Matthew, had coined a new word. Matthew used the Greek word, "epiosis" for the phrase, "daily bread" in the Lord's Prayer. Nowhere in all the scriptures, or in all the secular writing could this "epiosis" be found.

But, lo and behold, not too many years ago, some earthen jars were also found in the Holy Land. These jars contained parchments that were preserved and legible. The word "epiosis" appeared a large number of times. You see "epiosis" was merely a woman's shopping list! Food for the family, oil for the lamps, dry goods and such were the "epiosos."

"Oh, Ye Of Little Faith"!

NEW YEAR – NEW CREATURE

"Therefore if any man be in Christ,
he is a new creature; old things are
passed away; behold, all things are
become new."

II Cor. 5:17

New deal, new life, new start, new resolutions, new dawning – but, it surely seems the same somehow. The rotation of the earth is still at the same speed, length of days will certainly remain constant, and wars and rumors of wars are still our lot. There really hasn't been any drastic change. Yes, surely seems the same somehow.

Remember when Paul said, "Old things are passed away; behold, all things are become new." Have "all things" really become new? Has some of the "all" failed to materialize? Is the "all" incomplete?

As the Bible pictures these "all things" it would seem to portray a kind of Utopian arrangement. Even if some of these "all things" have not become new, surely this truth can be our reality. We can prove this promise.

God says, "Blessed is the man to whom the Lord will not impute sin." We know we have passed from condemnation. We have life. God has said our soul's salvation is sealed, saved and secured. Even with all this unerring assurance, our mortal lives may not be completely changed. The "all things" has not yet come to pass.

Could part of this incompleteness be correlated with our surrender? Have we given ourselves in unconditional surrender? Are we still waging warfare against our God?

Maybe some of our undoneness is "limited love." Could love parallel "all" in "all things"? Isn't love the magic ingredient so meaningful and so demanding in a Christian's make-up? Is love the "flour and body of the cake." or have we merely used it for "window-dressing" and "icing"?

Maurice Chevalier sang a song some years ago that says something to Christians. Listen: "I could work and slave the whole day through, if I could hurry home to you. You brought a new kind of love to me." Jesus certainly brought a new kind of love to us.

Then there is the area of service. Every Christian knows this. But just as surely as 2 and 2 are 4, the amount of service rendered to the King is directly proportional to the amount of surrender and love that are shown. Service is absolutely dependent on surrender and love. And are they not dependent on each other? They make up "all." Could this be in "all things"?

Now this phrase can reach its finest fulfillment and faithful fruition when surrender, love, and service are secured!

In closing, let us remember another "all things." Paul said, "I can do all things through Christ which strengtheneth me." Now, even this can be possible.

An old promise, a new year; yea, maybe even a new child of the King.

New Years Eve 1964

A DAY'S JOURNEY
LUKE 2:44

We are indebted to Dr. Luke for his tremendous insights into God's plans. No wonder he was entrusted to write about the "Acts of the Holy Spirit." In his first book, in the second chapter, he writes a wonderful thought-provoking episode. Leaving the birth of Jesus, Christmas and all the trappings, he writes about Mary and Joseph and Jesus on their journey to Jerusalem for the Feast of the Tabernacles. After the Feast, Luke writes, "They went a day's journey without Jesus." How can a loving mother and father misplace a twelve-year-old son? Didn't they love him? The Bible answers, "Yes." Weren't they concerned? Even with angels' visits, a flight into Egypt, and other protections, we have to say, "Sure, they were concerned." Why did they go a day's journey without Jesus? The answer is in the Book. It always is. It is because they supposed him to be in the crowd.

If Mary and Joseph can go a day's journey without Jesus, so can you and I. So can little cliques, small groups, churches, even denominations. How can we keep from going a day's journey without Jesus?

1. Check up on how we treat each other. We should be kind one to another because we never know what battle the other person is fighting.

2. Check up on the diet of our minds and the
   menu of our souls that can keep us from
   going a day's journey without Jesus.

None of the above solutions is enough. God's revelation is truly the best. Here it is: Just ask ourselves, "Is
my life pleasing to Jesus?" Allow the Holy Spirit who
lives within us to answer for us!

QUESTIONABLE MOTIVES

Many Christians and non-Christians have heard some very strange discussions about the wine at the Cana wedding feast. Some say alcoholic; some say non-alcoholic, some say denatured wine and so on.

Dear Hearts, if Jesus touched it, it was perfect! Leave it alone.

Then there was that occasion when Jesus drove the money changers from the temple. Some have doubts about the kind of anger Jesus displayed. Again, whatever He did was perfect! "The Servant is not greater than His Master." "No guile was found in His mouth."

He did say, "I and the Father are One." (Note the Plurality)

He also said, "I am the Way, the Truth, and the Life; no one comes to the Father except by Me."

Be careful about questioning motives! Feed your faith. Starve your doubts. Never forget in the dark what God has revealed in the light.

GOOD COMMON SENSE

The atomic scientist Albert Einstein said, "When you understand the essence of a thing, you can gain the knowledge to harness the power."

I maintain that if you even remotely understand the essence of God's love at Calvary and receive His Gift, you have already gained the knowledge and the good common sense to let the Power harness you!

BARRIERS

Barriers are things that separate us. Sometimes it is money, position, culture, color, education, or traditions.

I remember hearing a very high-positioned church leader say, "We are not going to give up 300 years of our church traditions for some people who crawled out of the bush." I immediately prayed, "Father forgive her." The statement she uttered was verbatim to what is written here. I say all the above to state this fact: "Love across the barriers is hard, especially if we love the barriers more than the people."

Thank God, there are no barriers with Jesus!

SATURDAY WAS DIFFERENT
(THE DAY AFTER
PRESIDENT KENNEDY'S ASSASSINATION)

Friday, November 22, 1963, was black and any other dark adjective befitting it – another infamous Friday; and Saturday was different.

The rain was rainier.
The smoke was blacker.
The trees were barer. But –
The church silhouette was surer, purer,
  promising eternal life.

Shock had now become grief. Rivers of tears had been shed. Jewish tears mingled with Catholic tears and Catholic tears mingled with Protestant tears. The black man grieved with the white man. The white man grieved with the brown man, and all grieved together.

"THE KING IS DEAD!" How trite and meaningless this used to be. When television news reels, radios, newspapers sounded the peal of foreign monarchs who had died. It seemed so irrelevant. But now, it hit home.

"THE PRESIDENT IS DEAD!"

This sound built into an engulfing Grand Canyon crescendo! It exploded in our minds and numbed us. We groaned in our tabernacles. We had anguish of soul.

My, but we must reap a harvest of lessons from this other infamous Friday and the empty gloom and defeat of Saturday. But what about Sunday? Sunday, the resurrection of Truth!

All our leaders now say, "Let us pray." Why not let our children pray? Why cannot our very lives be prayers? Our president gave his life for freedom and to free mankind. The Bible says, "Ye shall know the truth and the truth shall make you free!" Let us share this Truth with our fellow citizens.

November 23, 1963

QUIET TIME

Quiet time is being alone with the Lord and His word, at a special time and place. God created man for fellowship. He cherishes our quiet time; so should we. God's precious presence is crucial to our very lives.

The Bible is a great meeting place with God, and we can hear the voice of God through the word of God. In our quiet times His word comes alive.

We can share some of our innermost thoughts and secrets. He shares some things with us that are unique.

Quiet time is a time of refreshing and renewal, a time of "Getting our heads on straight," a time to see our place in His overall plan. Sometimes it is a sanctuary of solitude.

We choose the time, the place, the duration, and the frequency. God is always waiting and He is never too busy. God originated quiet time. Adam's best part of the day was his quiet time; it surely can be ours.

Quiet time comes highly recommended! It is here that we truly realize that we are loved!

"The supreme happiness of life is the conviction that we are loved." Victor Hugo

God Is Love!

INVALUABLE

"What would you give in exchange for your soul?" Jesus asks all of us this penetrating, revealing question. We would answer, "Everything." In fact, some of us would say, "All that we could borrow, beg, or steal."

Because every soul is so meaningful, irreplaceable, and will live forever, could Jesus also be asking, "What would you give in exchange for a soul?" A mate's soul, a child's, a grandchild's?" This question becomes very personal and of paramount importance!

Everyone deserves to hear the claims of Christ, the Good News. They need to hear it up close, eyeball to eyeball – heart to heart – soul to soul. People need to hear this because every soul is so precious. "God doesn't make any junk," and every soul is highly important to Him.

He continues to ask, "What would you give in exchange for your soul – for another's soul?"

We supply our own answers. With God's help, let us give our very best efforts. Jesus will affirm our endeavors with,

"Well Done."

(An Open letter to any and all Christian Fellowships
embarking on a witnessing Journey)

Dear Fellow Christians:

My heart is empathetically with you in your delibera-
tions. GOD IS SURELY GOING TO DO A MIGHTY
WORK THROUGH US*!* This is a faith statement, and the
entire universe groans to make a faith statement come true.
This world that was framed by a word is influenced by a
word.

It is definitely true that Jesus does all the saving! We
merely share the "Good News." But, it is equally true that as
Christians we each do as we "Want To," especially in relation to sharing our faith. THE KEY TO EFFECTIVE
EVANGELISM IS GETTING PEOPLE TO "WANT TO."
Just as in selling, we don't make people "buy" products or
services, we only make them "Want To."

Since the greatest thing that has happened to each of
us is Jesus coming into our lives, then doesn't it seem rea-
sonable that the second best thing is our sharing this "Good
News"? Witnessing for our Lord is an outgrowth of our love
for Him which blossoms from a grateful heart. We merely
need to make ourselves remember when we first met Jesus,
and experienced His great love. As we remember, we are
strangely warmed and willing to go forth and tell. This is
commitment. Commitment is 99% of an effectual personal
worker. Ability makes up the other 1%. In fact, the only ability that Jesus ever wants is our <u>availability</u>.

This commitment to anyone or anything, other than Jesus, will not suffice.

All the saints of the Old and New Testaments first had to stand up and promise the Lord they would go for him. Their commitments are recorded and real. This great life theme is of the HOLY SPIRIT. Commitment in its broadest sense is needed by Pastor and People if propagation of the Gospel is ever to be reached. "THE SPEED OF THE BOSS IS THE SPEED OF THE GANG."

Here is a series of axioms that definitely relates to soul winning:

- What you don't know you can't define or talk about.
- What you can't talk about you can't use.
- What you can't use you can't save.

This is absolutely pertinent to sharing the Gospel.

Lincoln once said, "We shall either meanly lose or nobly save man's last best hope." As fellow Christians, we can also say, "We are God's last best hope." And, we shall either meanly lose, like sniveling cowards, or nobly save, like children of the KING, God's last best hope.

I close with this FAITH STATEMENT, "WE SHALL NOBLY SAVE GOD'S LAST BEST HOPE."

THIS YEAR

Mend a quarrel
Seek out a forgotten friend
Share some treasure
Give a soft answer
Encourage youth
Keep a promise
Find the time
Listen
Apologize if you were wrong
Be gentle
Laugh a little
Laugh a little more
Express your gratitude
Welcome a stranger
Gladden the heart of a child
Take pleasure in the beauty and wonder of the earth
Speak your love
Speak it again
Speak it still once again.

Author Unknown

THE WAY

"I Am the way, the truth, and the life; . . ."
John 14:6

Christianity is a way, a walk, a highway, – narrow and straight, not crooked or curvy. Jesus threw no curves. His "pitches" were straight down the middle. "No guile was found in His mouth".

So Christianity is a <u>walk</u>, a daily walk with Christ. But it is much more. It is moving, vital, energizing, alive, conquering, sure, and the <u>way</u> that leads home.

Christianity is similar to a man climbing a glass hill. You climb – you slip. You climb some more. You must keep moving. For there is more than gold atop this "hill of life." Jesus is at the top! Peace, rest, eternal contentment, joys unspeakable await you there!

As you climb this hill of life, you will need help. Ask God. His counsel is true. His help is sure. His is the <u>only way!</u>

A LOVING FELLOWSHIP
(PARAMOUNT)

Hal B. Kuhnle was the epitome of grace in word and deed. He was pastor of Immanuel Baptist Church in Lexington, Ky., and was part of God's vision to move the church from a land-locked location in the city to 22 acres near a growing community. God put His stamp of approval on this and He blessed abundantly.

Catherine, his bride of many years, was a perfect helpmeet. Dignity and grace and kindness were their lot. They made all feel welcomed, wanted, needed, and loved.

Pastor Kuhnle shared with me a very poignant story that changed his life. He told me about a drunken man who called him many times one night. The drunk wanted the pastor to come to his home to talk to him. Pastor Kuhnle kept telling the man to come by his office in the morning. Later that night the man committed suicide. Pastor Kuhnle told me to always go where the need is. Difficulty is one excuse the Lord will not accept.

He taught me that the fellowship of the church is paramount. Jesus is very jealous of His Bride. No one person, no small group, no clique, and not even the pastor is more important than the fellowship!

The church was growing and going. There was no dissension whatsoever, and no trouble on the horizon. Then it happened! The pastor resigned! Only his wife was aware of his decision. His reason for resigning was very profound. He said the fellowship needed a younger, more energetic leader. He lived what he preached. Even though we all loved him we knew we could not dissuade him. Pastor Kuhnle will be remembered for a grace filled life. What a testimony! He knew and acted upon the best: "To glorify God and enjoy Him forever."

"It is impossible to govern
the world without
God and the Bible."

George Washington

ALL DAY A PRAYER

Three young seminary students had similar grades in school. They each served small nearby churches. Two of the young preachers were merely getting by in their fellowships. The other young student was having phenomenal success. His small church was growing by leaps and bounds.

The other two young preachers wanted to know why the third one was so successful. They followed him and they watched him. He ate what they ate, he studied what they studied, and his attendance in school was the same. The two curious young preachers decided it must be in his prayer life. They placed a ladder up to the window in the same dormitory they all lived in. They saw him come into his room and go to bed. The young successful preacher knelt down by his bed and merely said, "In Jesus' name, Amen!" His whole day had been a PRAYER!

Pray as though we aren't going to work.
Then work as though we aren't going to pray.

BLUEGRASS MIRACLES
HENRY HOLLEY

In the spring of 1971, Billy Graham and his team conducted a four day crusade in Lexington, Ky. It was a miracle-filled four days! Only eternity will reveal all the majesty and magnitude, and power of God that occurred during that crusade.

A few months before the actual meetings, I met a truly remarkable servant of the Lord, Henry Holley. At that time Henry managed the Montreat, N.C. office for Billy Graham. Henry, an ex-Marine, was a very imposing and efficient leader. He knows and lives more of God's word than any person I have ever met. We became fast friends. Henry allowed me to carry the boxes (an endearing expression) for the counselor training that he conducted. All that were involved learned much from Henry's classes. Shortly after the Lexington crusade, Billy Graham appointed Henry to be overseas crusade director. Henry is now serving Franklin Graham in a similar position.

Henry set up crusades in Korea, Japan, Hong Kong, Taiwan, Manila, Singapore, Rio de Janeiro, and many more.

Henry is under-girded, loved, and encouraged by his beautiful wife, Bettie. Their marriage of over 50 years is an inspiration to all.

They are true "Gems" for the Lord's Work!

BLUEGRASS MIRACLES
THE CRUSADE

The Central Kentucky Crusade in Lexington was conducted by Billy Graham and his team. A great spiritual revival occurred with many blessings for all the hundreds of volunteers and churches that participated.

I first met Billy Graham at a reception prior to the crusade. I invited Billy and T.W. Wilson to a golf game. Billy readily accepted and asked me to get Bob Denny, President of Baptist World Alliance, to join us as our "fourth." When we played, I drove the golf cart for Billy and myself. The fellowship was exhilarating and the entire occasion a much treasured memory.

The crusade was held in the basketball coliseum which seated about 15,000 people. On Sunday afternoon 35,000 showed up! We moved 20,000 to the north stand of Stoll Field, the football stadium, adjacent to the coliseum. A platform on the 50 yard line was about 100 feet into the football field. The sound system was excellent so all could hear.

Before the program started, Billy Graham and about 10 of his team members came to the platform. Billy welcomed everyone and commented that it was much nicer there than in the hotter coliseum. Then he did an amazing thing! He introduced me to the audience and told them that I would conduct the invitation after the end of the message. I was the most startled person in the whole world! I am not a preacher or the son of a preacher, but just a layman who loves Jesus.

The stadium audience sang along with the coliseum choir and listened intently to Billy's message which was powerful and inviting. The Holy Spirit was completely in charge. When the invitation was given, the choir started singing, "Just As I Am," and folks started streaming out of the stands towards the platform where I stood with the microphone. Over 2,000 people responded. I asked all who wanted Christ to come into their lives, to forgive them, and to save them, to come to the platform. After the people had gathered around the platform, I assured them that God was pleased with their coming. I asked them to repeat after me a sinner's prayer. They did so very loudly, and you could actually hear an echo from the opposite stands. It was as though God was approving their commitments. I then told them they had made the wisest choice of their lives and that there were many pastors and counselors in their midst to give them materials and to help them on their journey with Jesus. As I matched up people in small groups with counselors. I realized we needed more help. The sound truck people called over to the coliseum for extra counselors and 200 more arrived and began helping with the new converts.

My pastor, Dr. Ted Sisk, was one of the additional counselors who came over from the coliseum. Almost all of the people who did not come forward stayed seated in the stands as they wanted to be witness to the great miraculous outpouring of the Holy Spirit.

After a while, my pastor made his way to the edge of the platform; where I was standing and I leaned down to hear what he wished to say. He told me that over in the coliseum my son, Robert, was one of the first to come forward to make his public profession of faith. Wow! I said, "Thank you Lord, thank you, thank you, thank you." I realized you cannot out give the Lord for He also says, "The laborer is worthy of his hire." (Luke 10:7)

I also learned this primary truth: God can save whomever, wherever, however, and whenever. And the results are forever! His promises are true! "For whosoever shall call upon the name of the Lord shall be saved." (Romans 10:13)

The ultimate goal is to glorify God and to enjoy Him forever!.

PONDER THIS

"He who converts a soul,
Draws water from a fountain;
But he who trains
A soul winner,
Digs a well
From which thousands
May drink to eternal life."

– Spurgeon

Highly recommended **must read** books –
Doing Time by Rick Nielson and Ron Kuntz
"Crime, America's Second Vietnam"
by Bill Glass and Terry Pluto

THROUGH THEIR EYES

"Sometimes we can see a person's heart
through their eyes."
"The eyes are the windows of the soul."
"It's hard to lie through your eyes."

"Three luxuries that a Christian can not afford:
self-pity, vindictiveness and hard feelings"

BRIC-A-BRAC

God gave us the Holy Spirit not just for our "enjoyment," but for our "employment."

Gifts we make today will impact someone's tomorrow, even their eternity!

Sometimes we have to go thru the thorn room to get to the throne room.

Difficulty is one excuse the Lord will not accept.

There is nothing more pitiful than a half-filled Christian trying to overflow.

Removing your halo will take a lot of weight off your mind.

Our heartbeats are numbered, what are we spending them on?

Best heart exercise is reaching down and helping someone up.

A satisfied need is not a motivator. (Sometimes it is difficult to witness to the wealthy.)

There is no such thing as "constructive criticism." Criticism is criticism. Period.

Ignorance of the Bible is ignorance of Jesus.

A faith that fizzled had a flaw from the first.

Christianity is an "all-the-time thing", not just "a-once-in-a-while thing."

Don't pray for a lighter load. Pray for a stronger back.

The Bible is a great meeting place with God. We can hear the voice of God thru the Word of God.

What did Jesus say about judging? "Don't".

What part of "don't", don't we understand?

Let God be as original with the other person as He is with us.

Discipline, not desire, determines destiny.

Never forget in the dark what God has revealed in the light.

Be kind to everyone. We don't know what kind of battles they are fighting.

The accent of love will penetrate where the tones of anger could never find a way.

Since this God that we know and love and serve even goes to the funeral of a sparrow, you can bet your bottom dollar, God will hear you when you cry out to Him!

If we leave Jesus un-discovered, we will leave life's vital issues unattended. The most vital is eternity!

There was forgiveness in the heart of God, long before there was sin in the heart of man.

"I'm convinced that what we keep owns us, and what we give away sets us free".   (Rev. Martin Luther Agnew)

TWO ENDS

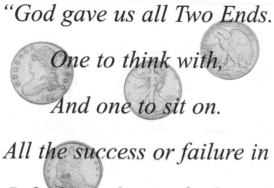

"God gave us all Two Ends.

One to think with,

And one to sit on.

All the success or failure in

Life depends on which end

You use.

Heads you Win!

Tails you Lose!"

Author Unknown

WHY GO TO PRISONS?

A correct short answer is we go because "we want to." There is a great need.

A recent Washington report said one in every 32 adults in the United States was behind bars or on probation or parole by the end of 2002. They found a record 6.6 million people in the nation's correctional system. "The overall figures suggest that we have come to rely on the criminal justice system as a way of responding to social problems in a way that's unprecedented," said Marc Mauer, assistant director of the sentencing project. He also said, "We are setting new records every day."

Prisons are great "fishing holes." Jesus said, "I'll make you fishers of men." We can catch two on a hook. Also, you do not have to spend three days and three nights to try to convince the inmates that they have a great need. The vacuums in their lives attest to this. The prison walls speak volumes. Our very presence in the prisons says, "We care." Everyone can use a new friend who will listen as well as talk. Another reason for our going is because, "holler for holler and dollar for dollar" it's a very profitable method to enhance God's Kingdom.

But probably the best answer to why we go is because the Lord Himself wants us to. He did say,

"I WAS IN PRISON AND YOU VISITED ME."

It's as though God is saying to all of us who have the Good News, "I'm giving you one last chance; give it your best shot. I am about to close up shop."

Praise The Lord!

LETTERS FROM INMATES

It's Raining Here

"It's raining here," one inmate wrote. "We are locked in our cells, but I can see out on the yard where the Bill Glass program was held. I can even see second base on the ball field. I go by there every day and pray for you. It was there you told me about Jesus and I trusted Him."

A Hug

"Bob, you probably don't remember me, but I am the big fellow with all the tattoos. You came over to the weight pile to visit some of us. You asked us, "Did you see and hear the program?" We said, We did. Some of us were strangely interested. You shared some more with us and asked if we would like to pray with you and ask God to forgive us and give us Jesus as Lord and Savior. I remember I only nodded, Yes. We prayed! You told us that if you really meant that prayer that you are more eternal than the moon and the sun and the stars! Then you gave me a big hug. No man had ever hugged me before. I would have stuck a knife in him. I can still feel your arms around me. You made me feel important. It was like Jesus hugging me! Praise His Holy Name."

The accent of love will penetrate where the tones of anger could never find a way.

THIRTY YEARS IN PRISON

This sounds like a long time, but it truly has sped by. I have not and will not regret one day of it! I, like so many others, have done countless things that I regret, but there are three things I will never regret:

1) I'll never regret trusting Christ as my Savior.
2) I'll never regret being a cheerful giver.
3) I'll never regret answering the prison call.

Rehabilitation doesn't work; only regeneration is successful. After 350 Weekends and over 2000 prisons and untold blessings, I've discovered some things and God has revealed some things about prisons and prisoners.
- In the first place, "We do what we want to."
- Everything we do stems from our own self image (there are many things that contribute to our self image)
- Poor father image (Home is where life makes up its mind about everything that matters.)
- No blessing from the fathers (Bill Glass message on "The Blessing" should be compulsory for every family, everywhere)
- A very detrimental, debilitating thing that can truly destroy ones self-image is this: "a sense of being cheated." Real or imaginary, it is the same.

This is ingrained into some folks. They hear this idea of being cheated and "taking the worst of it" from a lot of sources. They hear it at home, at play, at school, even in their churches, and most of all from their so-called "leaders". This is a hurtful stigma and a heavy burden. There is a sense that "the world owes me and I'm going to get what's mine." All this sets up and makes for a poor self-image. This is a common denominator for inmates. My heart goes out to folks who have been "steered" on this devastating course! But, here again, we do what we want to. "The "want to's" must be changed! Only Jesus can do this!

IS IT WORTH IT?

This great God-motivated movement of going into prisons, is it worthwhile? You bet your "bottom dollar," it's worth it. The reasons and results speak volumes!

* * * For all who participate, the blessings are terrific.
* * * It is great "on the job" training for all.
* * * We become better parents and citizens.
* * * Our lives are fuller and richer.

For the prison systems the results are very profitable.

* * A great calming influence comes over the prisons.
* * The number of "write-ups" or disciplinary
     reports shrinks dramatically.
* * Management is much easier for the
     correctional officers.
* * There is a tremendous financial savings!

Recidivism is normally about 67 percent, but with committed Christian inmates the recidivism drops to under 10 percent. This leaves a 57 percent bonus in recidivism. A quick extrapolation of 60,000 inmates that do not return to prison, times an average of $30,000 per year warehouse costs, and we have a savings of one billion eight hundred million dollars – a lot of money. Enormous amounts of money have been saved through the efforts of "Weekend of Champions" and "Day of Champions." Another wonderful plus is the great number of productive citizens with changed lives, who do not return to prisons.

All in all, the prison ministry makes for a safer and more free country. No wonder that "Champions for Life" are receiving more invitations into prisons than they can accept. Yet, with God all things are possible.

Another Opportunity
Is The Reward
For A
Job Well Done!

PURE CONJECTURE

Conjecture means to infer by inconclusive evidence; to throw together.

About the same time the Bill Glass prison ministry began, a great happening was occurring in. . . Wilmore, Kentucky, a small town just a few miles from Lexington, and home of Methodist Asbury College. A wonderful saint of God, Dr. David Seamonds, pastored the major church, United Methodist. God had sent a Holy Spirit led revival. I shared there a couple of times and I saw with my own eyes and felt it with my heart. Very few of the surrounding churches latched onto the wonder and power of this Wilmore Revival.

The following is pure conjecture:

There is a strong possibility that this great movement of God leap-frogged into the prisons of America through the "Total Person Weekends with Bill Glass and Friends." Dr. David Seamonds and his brother, J.T., were two of our very early Spiritual Enrichment speakers. (We have an hour or more with a speaker on Friday mornings before we enter the prisons.) God has blessed in a most supernatural way in each prison we've visited with thousands and thousands of commitments.

There have been dozens of satellite ministries spring up by folks who shared in these prison weekends. This phenomenon continues. The revival burns brighter, especially since 9 11. Revivals thrive in crisis situations and every-one in prison is in crisis.

It's as though God is saying to all of us who have the Good News, "I'm giving you one last chance; give it your best shot. I am about to close up shop."

Praise The Lord!

WEEKEND OF CHAMPIONS

A FITTING TITLE

Inmate rehabilitation in the corrections systems is totally ineffective. The recidivism rate remains about 70 percent with or without rehabilitation. There needs to be a better solution. There is. It's regeneration! The fact of regeneration is the prime mover and motive behind "Weekend of Champions." The focus in on the incarcerated, both young and old. In all the hundreds of prisons that the Weekend of Champions has visited, there has never been a serious incident. On the contrary, there is always a calming influence. "Dollar for dollar and holler for holler," it is a beautiful and efficient way to share the gospel.

A Weekend of Champions is well structured. It has a committed God-fearing leadership with many dedicated helpers. The invitations come from governors, wardens, and superintendents. Then there is a thorough checkout of the prisons and dates are set. Motels are secured. Coordinators, transportation, schedules, platform guests, and the heart of the ministry, the teammates all meet for the scheduled WOC. The logistics are overwhelming, but the Holy Spirit is in charge. The entire operation goes like clock work. The coordinators and their groups of teammates, who are trained, equipped, and prayed up, go to their specific prisons. The platform guests adhere to their schedules. God blesses the programs, the plan, the people, and the purpose on each occasion. The victory is His!

COORDINATORS

Coordinators do precisely as their name implies. They are the "go between" for the prison officials and the team-mates and the platform guests. They also are the final authority for their group of Dedicates.

These leaders, both men and women always manage in love. They are winsome, great communicators, and pleasant but firm. They have a wonderful overview of God's plan.

They rise early and stay up late. Each one always does a final check-out of their specific institution on Thursday. They make sure of the details such as the program areas, timing of programs, sound systems and many things to make sure all goes smoothly.

They are the cadre for the rest of the troops. But they serve with kindness and grace having come up thru the ranks themselves. On some occasions they perform as "mother hens."

These leaders surely must be the authors of the eleventh commandment, "thou shall be flexible – don't get bent out of shape."

Coordinators have courage as their middle name. They would actually "beard a lion in his den." You see, they always trust and depend upon the Lord and His Promises.

Many of our coordinators say, "I am at my best when I am ministering in prison." Innovating, and training and teaching and managing and ministering are part and parcel of the coordinators. They always,

"Go The Second Mile."

PLATFORM GUESTS

Some of the Weekend of Champions platform guests have included Tom Landry, Reggie White, Bruce Collie, Roger Staubach, "Mean" Joe Green, Billy "White Shoes" Johnson, Earl Campbell, Bob Breunig, John Niland, Tommy Johns, Michael Jordan, Dave Washington, Mike McCoy, Harold Thompson, McCoy McLemore, and wonderful musicians and singers. Many other world-class athletes have been our platform guests. They are all Champions for Christ and have learned the difference between "celebrities" and "servants." They share as servants.

An example: McCoy McLemore shows the inmates his world championship ring he won with the Milwaukee Bucks. His favorite story, and he tells it well, is an Old Persian Proverb.

"He who knows not, and knows not that he knows not, is a fool – shun him; He who knows not and knows that he knows not is a child – teach him; He who knows, and knows not that he knows, is asleep – wake him; He who knows and knows that he knows is wise – follow him."

McCoy has also served thirty years in prisons. He is a very dear and trusted friend. But best of all, he is a friend of Jesus!

Other friends of Jesus who have served as platform guests are Paul Wrenn, the world's strongest man; "Murph the Surf"; Tanya Crevier, the world's best basketball handler; Ron Kuntz, world renowned photographer; Bunny Martin, world champion yo-yo- expert; Tino Wallenda of high-wire fame; Rick Nielsen, world class magician and motivator; and, of course, our leader and founder, Bill Glass. It would consume too much time and space to list all Bill's accomplishments, other than to say he is God's man for America's prisons.

TEAMMATES

God has an army of upwards of 37,000 or more teammates, and the army keeps growing. These are our front line troops, who truly are the heart of the ministry. They come in all shapes and sizes, and flavors. They even pay their own expenses. They come by cars, planes, buses, and motorcycles. Some even come by hitchhiking, but mainly, they come.

Bill Glass says that they are not volunteers; they are "Dedicates." Volunteers pick their place of service. God picks the place of service for "Dedicates."

The entire ministry of "Champions for Life" is one large wholesome family with no fighting. In over 30 years with the Ministry, I've never heard or heard about a quarrel amongst our teammates. We have one goal in mind, one purpose, one passion – to "share Christ in the power of the Holy Spirit, and leave the results up to God."

Neither weather, the logistics, the conditions, the toughness of the situation, nor any other obstacle seems to deter our teammates from their appointed and anointed tasks. They show up for the "Divine Encounters." They are members of churches who pray diligently and "put feet on their prayers." They come from all walks of life and they gladly go the second mile. They have learned well some salient truths. There are no "big time operators", "middle-sized operators" or "small time operators" in God's world. We are all equal. We believe, "God so loved the World," and He is no respecter of persons.

At our banquets, when I look at the hosts of team-mates, I don't see any kings; I don't see any king makers; but my, my, my, I do see hosts of kingdom makers. I'm certain that our Savior is pleased!

NO ATTACK – NO DEFENSE

No attack – no defense is the philosophy for the "Champions of Life" and "The Weekend of Champions." We are warned in the "Do's and Don'ts" as part of the training, never to criticize any religion, and never to tell anyone they are going to hell. We are admonished to keep positive and on track with the gospel, period.

Many thousands of folks whose lives have been changed by Jesus will attest to this philosophy. Our very presence in the prisons says very dramatically, "We care."

Our philosophy remains the same –"No attack – No defense."

LOGISTICS

The Weekend of Champions people are invited guests in the prisons. We adhere to the rules. We do not try to tell them how to run their business. Our three top priorities are the same as theirs, security, security, security.

After all the preliminaries, there is God's army that has to be assembled, trained, equipped, and transported to the front lines in the prisons. (Lucifer's strongholds)

It took our troops in "Operation Iraqi Freedom" four whole days to reach the outskirts of Baghdad. This was a record. They did have some supply problems. It takes God's army who come from all over America about a day and a half to come out of their comfort zones to the front lines in the prisons. They do not have any supply problems. Our warriors have put on the full armor, with plenty of swords and ammunition, well trained, and fully equipped. We even have a mechanized division, the Christian Motorcyclists, with their fancy shining bikes and their colorful outfits. We are reminded of the phrase, "the cohorts were gleaming in silver and gold," from Byron's "Destruction of Sennacherib."

The motorcyclists' leader, Don Johnson, says to the inmates, "I love you and there is not a thing you can do about it".

Incidentally, there are no casualties in God's army. They are always victorious!

His Word Is Alive

HOME COUNTS

"Home is where life makes up its mind about everything that matters." This becomes very evident when you examine the backgrounds of people. There is a real correlation between a bad home life and inmates. This phenomenon is a common denominator.

There is a startling statistic with upwards of 90,000 inmates in a large state, only 27 Jewish men could be found in the system. There were thousands of "Christians," both Catholic and Protestant. There were many, many other religions, but there were only 27 Jewish men. There is something good to say about Bar Mitzvah and Jewish home life. They also receive the blessings from their fathers. All of us could learn from this phenomenon. Of course, if we are too smug in our thinking, and say, "Don't bug me with facts," then the trend will continue.

After speaking at a Rotary Club on one occasion, a Jewish rabbi invited me to speak to his congregation. I readily accepted. I told him my best friend was a rabbi. He asked me who, and I answered, "Jesus."

What we know of Jesus' home life, we can all agree it was good. Hc had great training. Even the scriptures tell us to be like Jesus. "Let the mind of Christ be in you."

A Godly Home Really Counts.

JAILHOUSE DAYS

Jailhouse days and jailhouse nights
Jailhouse store calls that cause jailhouse fights.
I think of family & where I should be
& know the jailhouse is not for me!
You meet lots of people just like you,
Bored to death with nothing to do
They sit and they dream of a man with a key.
That fits a door to set them free.
I sit & I wonder with each day to come
If I'll ever get back to the ones I love.
You sit & you think of the friends that you have,
The money they owe you & the laughs that you've had.
You think of your wife & who she is with.
Is he a stranger or is he a friend?
You think of your children, each & every day
& hope they're not hurt at school or at play.
You think of your animals, your furry little friends
& hope they are fed and petted again.
But you know in your mind & you know in your heart
All of these things are a world apart.
So when you think of all this & you think it is the end,
Just open your heart & let Jesus in.
For when you do this you shall see
There was never a door that needed a key.
So put all your worries in His merciful hands
Cause if you didn't know it He had it all planned.

"The Gypsy"

A FREE CRIME

A few years ago I had an interesting conversation with a California warden. He remembered the Bill Glass team from different prisons in his state.

We are admonished to be courteous to all officers, even rookies, in the prison systems. One day they will be captains or majors or even wardens.

So, this warden in California and I were reminiscing, and he asked me, "How many of these weekends have you done, Bob?" I said about 350. He next said, "Oh my, you have a free crime coming." I assured him that I am still in debt. All of us who claim Christ as our Savior are in debt! Although, we could never pay it off, it truly is a lot of fun trying.

"It only takes a moment to become a Christian,
it takes a lifetime of being one!"

VISIT IN PSYCHO WARD

During a Weekend of Champions, I was assigned to have a short program in the mental ward in Oklahoma. I thought all went well with the program. That evening at the "snack and share" time, the Coordinator for that prison gave a report. He told about the mental ward and said one of the inmates came up to him "grinning like a Cheshire cat" and said, "We sure did like old Bob; he's one of us."

WHAT I TELL INMATES

Since I am aware of the crisis situation, poor self-image or self-esteem or self-worth of my audience, I tell them certain things that they "need" to hear. I don't tell them what they want to hear, but what they truly "need" to hear. But first I earn the right to share with them. I usually do a card trick and maybe throw a card or two over a wall or fence. I do this for two reasons: 1) for entertainment; and 2) to develop credentials. I remember a few occasions when I threw a card over the wall, I'd have a lot of volunteers wanting to go get it for me. After some levity and using some inmates in the "magic party", I've earned their respect and their attention. I never preach. We leave this up to the preachers. From my heart I share some truths.

1. I usually ask them, "Why did you come to the program?" We get the correct answer. They say they came because they wanted to. I say, "So did I, because I wanted to. If I were in here I'd want someone to come and rap with me."

2. Sometimes I use Don Johnson's phrase, "I love you and there is not a thing you can do about it. I love you and God loves you . . . that's a majority." Sometimes I tell them I am older than dirt. I just use a lot of make-up.

3. I explain to them that in the sight of God, there are no big dudes, middle-sized dudes or small dudes. God loves all the same and no matter what any of us have done, it does not enter the equation. God loves us. I found out a long time ago that the "accent of love will penetrate where the tones of anger could never find a way."

4. I tell them, "I don't know how you feel. The officers don't know how we feel . . .the psychiatrists don't know how we feel. Only we know how we feel! So let's put our cards on the table face up."

5. "I can identify with folks who have been 'put down'. We have heard some of the prosecutor's remarks and some of the judges scathing terms. They seem to try to make us feel like we are a big zero. Well, I've got some precious news for us. We are not zeros, you and I. Instead of being a zero, every last one of us in the sound of my voice is a 200 million to one shot. Here is the scientific proof. Realize that before the egg in your mother's womb was fertilized, that there were 200 million sperm cells trying to fertilize that egg. But only one made it.

You, you, you, and me. The one with the soul.
God does not make junk! God does not book
any flops. When He made us, He did it right.
"Let Us make man in Our own image". Each
one of us is unique in the entire world. We are
one of a kind. God says we are highly important to Him. He says we are special! I say
YOU are special. My teammates say you are
are special or we wouldn't be here. God has
a plan for you. You have taken the worst of it
all your life and it is high time for a change".

6. I share a very short testimony. I ask the inmates
   to huddle with my teammates. My teammates
   share the "Four Laws" and many of the inmates
   pray for salvation! God gets the glory!

NO GAME PLAYING

An integral part of my message to the inmates is this, "You can't play any games on the Lord." How are you going to play a game on someone so brilliant, so powerful, that said, "Let there be light", and there was light. "Let there be worlds", and there were worlds. "Let there be people", and there were people. He is too sharp for us. How are we going to con someone who has the video tape on us – all of our past, all of our present, all of our future. Shame on us.

When the game is all over, <u>He</u> is going to win. I want all of us to be with Him on the winning team. We don't have to carry the ball or the water either. I just want all of us to be on the traveling squad. God wants the same thing. You and you alone make the choice, your own choice! Forget the games. God loves you and I love you. This is a majority.

We can't fret over the past mistakes. God will put them as far away as "the East is from the West." God's Word in Hebrews chapter 11 has a catalog of some of His saints. The list includes multiple murderers, liars, con men, thieves, and even a madam, since Rahab owned a house.

There were all sorts of sinners. Is that to say that God takes people like these and makes saints out of them? That is precisely what He does! He still wishes to do the same for any of us.

Praise His Name – Forget The Games!

WAUPUN

In the spring of 1974, Bill Glass and about 36 lay-men descended upon the prison in Waupun, Wisconsin. This was a maximum security compound in the middle of this small town. There had been a riot some five years before and only half of the inmates were allowed on the yard at a time. The warden, Ray Gray, decided to stay the entire weekend to check out these "do-gooders" and to make sure of the security – the top priority for them and us.

On Friday, late in the afternoon, Bill Councilman, the prison chaplain, and I were talking. He told me about a young 25 year old African American who was the "leader" in this prison. We agreed to pray that God would move on his heart. This young man was the toughest dude in prison. He was about 6'8" and all muscle. Immediately after pray-ing, and not two feet from Bill and me stood this young man, Henry Lewis. Bill said to me, "Bob, meet Henry Lewis." I said, "Thank you, Lord, hello, Henry". I asked Henry if I could share the little gold book with him. Henry answered, "Yes, but I want you to do something for me first." I asked him what is it. He pointed out a correction officer who had just put him "on report". He asked me to go talk to the officer. I did. I began by introducing myself to the officer and said, "I know we have caused some con-cern and some confusion. It's probably mostly our fault that Henry didn't line up and respond correctly earlier (that was the offense). I also told the officer that I was on vaca-tion and had some more time left on my vacation. I said,

"If I could, I would like to serve Henry's time in the hole for his infraction". The officer said, "You'd do that for him?" I agreed. Then the officer said he would take his name off the report, but I should tell Henry to shape up. I agreed. Henry heard all this and he asked, "Why would you do such a thing?" I said, "Henry, let me tell you about my best friend and how He took my place." Henry gave his heart to Jesus. Henry then became our very best booster and cheerleader! Even the warden got saved! So did many of his officers. God truly had a field day!

We returned to Waupun fifteen years later. Bill Glass Bible Studies and follow-up were still going strong.

"And I pray that as you share your faith with others, it will grip their lives too as they see the wealth of good things in you that come from Christ Jesus."

Philemon 6th Verse Living Bible

DEATH ROW

Some of the prisons have death rows. Our visits to them are always very memorable. In 2002 some of us spent an entire Saturday in a major death row. We went from cell to cell. Nearly everybody we visited wanted to talk to us. They got very few visits. There was only one person per cell. We never ask about their crimes. We do not want anything to get in the way of sharing the gospel.

I usually introduce myself and shake hands with the inmate through the food slot in his cell door. I begin our talk by telling the inmate that I don't know how you feel. This seems to be a good honest start. I met quite a few men in this particular building who knew the Lord, who were just waiting His return. They seemed very contented. I recall one man told me that he had been on death row for 27 years. He was completely at ease. He was also a student of the scriptures. I probably visited too long with him.

I shall never forget what one young man told me after I said, "I don't know how you feel." He said, "Bob, I don't have any feelings." I had never heard that before. I said, "Son, you are not a zombie, you are real flesh and blood." I continued, "Jesus loves you and I love you." How do you feel about that?" He said, "I feel much better."

I was extremely patient with him. I shared the little gold book, The Four Laws. He was completely immersed in this encounter with the Living Lord. He anxiously prayed to receive Christ as his Savior and Lord. I gave him my New Testament. The men on both sides of his cell were also believers. The fellowship began immediately. God is faithful!

UNTIL YOU'VE BEEN ARRESTED

Until you've been arrested, spent countless days in jail,
Walked a thousand miles but never left your cell,
Until you've lost your friends, you're lonely and all alone,
You search your heart for comfort, but comfort is all gone.
Until you've seen a judge and entered a guilty plea, and heard
The words of judgment, that you're never going to be free,
Until the days have turned to months,
and the months have turned to years,
You lay awake at night, shedding worthless tears.
Until you've lost all hope and every dream you've had
You fight to keep your sanity, to keep from going mad.
Until you've done all this, and lost all human will,
Don't ever try to tell me that you know how I feel!

Billy Ray

ALABAMA DEATH ROW

This is about a wonderful experience on Alabama's Death Row. The warden and I go back to 1979. He said, "Bob, do you have any time to visit death row?" I had an hour and a half between programs. He escorted me to the library section of death row. There were 20 men diligently studying and researching the law books. They were trying to find something, anything, to give them hope.

The warden introduced me. I immediately began doing some magic, like multiplying coins, and a mystifying card trick. I asked them to huddle up around me so they could see better. All the time I was sharing what God had done for me and what he wanted to do for them. Three skin heads were in the audience. They kept asking me what I thought about the death penalty. I told them my leaders would not let me discuss this. All the time I kept telling them about the love of Jesus. What any of us do or do not do does not enter the equation. I shared the gospel the best way I knew how. I asked the entire group if they were willing to pray a sinner's prayer with me. There were no objections. The three skin heads moved away from the group. We prayed. As soon as we finished praying, four of my teammates appeared. They made their own small huddles with the 17 inmates who had prayed. God will provide! "Jehovah Jaireh".

SCOOTER

The Weekend of Champions had been invited into the Texas Prisons. It was the last program on Saturday afternoon in the women's unit. The program area was a basketball court with a truck bed for a platform. It seemed the entire population of women inmates and officers were there. The inmates had been witnessed to on Friday and all day Saturday. Much seed had been sown and watered. At the end of the speaking, we matched up our teammates in huddles with the inmates. God was having a field day.

Not in any of the huddles was a very masculine looking woman, named Scooter. She was more or less the boss or leader of the prison. She was double tough, or you might say, "tough as a pine knot." I walked over to her and we started talking. I did most of the listening, but I surmised she was ready for a change in her life. I told her about a friend who was a harlot in New Orleans. My friend, Iris's testimony goes like this. She said, "I knelt down as a whore and prayed, and stood up as a princess." This was the key for Scooter to unlock her heart. She knelt down on the concrete and prayed and repented and asked Jesus to save her. She also stood up as a princess. Many of the inmates saw her. Many hugged her, with a different kind of hug. Scooter was crying and so were some of us.

The Angels In Heaven Were Rejoicing!

HE KEEPS TELLING

In April of 1979, the Weekend of Champions visited Atmore, Alabama prisons. The officers were very cooperative. We were allowed to visit every inmate including those on death row. Twelve of us went to death row and spent half a day sharing Christ. God's grace is still amazing.

I recall a very memorable and blessed visit. The first inmate I talked to had a log chain padlocked around his cell door. I never had seen this type of security. His name was John Evans. He came from a very respected middle class family. He did not fit any mold for the average prisoner. I never asked him about his crime, but the news media was extremely interested in his case. He said he did not want anyone to interfere with his execution. He insisted that no one, not family or lawyers or anyone, try to get him a stay of execution. This was national news. I introduced myself to him and said I was with the Bill Glass group. He said, "Just a minute. I received a letter from a young girl in Ohio who said she was with the "Friend of a Prisoner" program. I told him that God loves him and so do I or we wouldn't be here. He said, "That's strange. Those are the same words that the Catholic priest said just a few minutes ago." Coincidences began piling up. He moved closer to the bars so we could communicate better. All the time we were talking, Ron Kuntz, a UPI photographer, was taking pictures of us. Evans and I were oblivious to Ron. We were both engrossed in the little gold book, <u>The Four Laws.</u> In about ten minutes John Evans was on his knees telling God he was sorry for his sins and asking Jesus to come into his heart. God is faithful. Ron's pictures were in newspapers all over America.

John and I communicated by letter for five years. John conducted prayer meetings and Bible studies on death row for all those years. John's appeals ran out! He received a date for his execution. Even the members of the family he had wronged appealed to spare his life. Many of us wrote and wired the Governor . . .all to no avail. Two evenings before John's execution, the very same priest who first told John God loved him, visited in John's cell near the execution chamber. The priest was allowed to videotape a short message from John. It is entitled, "Dead Wrong." It has been shown by CBS many times even on prime time. Thousands of copies of this tape are being used in prisons and youth centers all over the world. John is still telling about the love, mercy, and grace of our blessed Savior.

AMAZING GRACE

Sometimes in the prisons, we are permitted to have programs on Death Row. In a North Carolina prison in 1982, they allowed 62 death row inmates to assemble in one large totally secured day room. Eight of our Champions For Life had the program for the inmates. We merely showed up as, "hitchhikers with Jesus." It was His idea, His plan, His words, and His program. All of us agreed that it was all of Him and none of us. At the end of the program there were many commitments to Christ. There was one young man standing aloof against a cell door. I made my way to him. He was bare-chested with a motorcycle tattoo on his chest. I asked him why he did not seem to want to be involved with Jesus. He said he was tired of "running games on people." I assured him God was pleased with his honesty. In a few moments, he fell to his knees and told God he was sorry and asked for forgiveness. Before he could get off his knees, the whole group was singing, "Amazing Grace". There were chill bumps on top of chill bumps! We still believe that the angels of heaven were leading the singing.

Twenty years later in 2002, I spoke on the yard at another North Carolina Prison. After I had shared and matched up our teammates with the inmates in huddles, I stepped off the platform. A fine looking young man asked me, "Bob, do you remember me?" I said, "I can't remember". He bared his chest and I recognized the motorcycle tattoo. We hugged and hugged. He told me his sentence had been commuted to life in prison. He said, "Bob, don't worry about me, I am now the Chaplain's assistant." He said, "It looks like we are going to have a lot of work to do with these new babies in Christ." He told me that he will come up for parole in 2024. Thank God for that wonderful reunion. I assured my brother in Christ, "I will see you, here, there, or in the air." But guaranteed and proof positive we will be together again. What a grand reunion awaits us! It will happen because of:

Gods Amazing Grace!

WALLA WALLA WONDERS

Some years ago during a Weekend of Champions in Walla Walla, Washington, I met one of God's choicest co-workers. His first name was George. He invited me to come back to Walla Walla to share in a couple of fund raisers for two downtown rescue missions that he managed. One was in Walla Walla and one was in Pasco. Hundreds of people were being fed in each facility, fed with food and fed with God's love.

The mission in Walla Walla was a very large two story warehouse with 12 small apartments on the top floor. Most of the bottom floor was used as a kitchen, a large eating area, and sleeping area with cots. The town's people funded the operation expenses through their yearly fund raisers.

The Friday evening banquet was attended by the Mayor, Chief of Police, Sheriff, and many business and church leaders. The giving response was very generous. It was 6 figures for each event, both Friday and Saturday. It was God's will that we all gave. All of the funds were used very wisely and were accounted for.

The banquets were tremendous blessings, but the most memorable event occurred Saturday morning. In the Walla Walla Mission on Saturday, a few hundred of the homeless attended for the scrumptious breakfast served with a large cookie as a treat. Before we ate, we were asked to gather into small groups for a ten minute prayer session. Nearly all complied. I noticed a few American Indians in the back of the room were not involved, and so I sauntered over to this group. I was immediately told by their spokesman, Hawk, that they had their own way of praying and worshiping. He said their religion was much older than Christianity. I listened very intently, and assured him I respected all he said, and just wanted to make new friends. I had never had the privilege of being friends with real American Indians.

We shook hands all around and then it was time for breakfast. I asked them if I could eat with their group and they said yes. I offered Hawk my cookie and it disappeared into his small back pack. I told him George had asked me to share a few words after breakfast. Hawk said, "I have to go now." I told him that if he were going to speak, I would stay and listen because that is what friends do. He said, "O.K., I'll stay." I did a couple of magic tricks to break the ice, and then I shared my story. The Holy Spirit had full sway of the meeting. We had an invitation, and the first persons to come forward were Hawk and two of his friends. I went to meet him and we hugged. The Lord continued to bless. Many precious souls were born into God's Kingdom that day. God is faithful!

Later I was told Hawk went to work for George at the mission. One of the apartments became available for Hawk, his wife, and their little papoose. Jehovah Jireh – God will provide.

God has something very special for my friend George. God says through Paul, ". . what makes me happiest is the well-earned reward you will have because of your kindness."

Philippians 4:17 Living Letters

Walla Walla was truly full of wonders!

GLAD I WAS IN PRISON

"I'm glad I was in prison," say hundreds of inmates. All of my teammates have heard this statement over and over again. Why would anyone in their right mind say such a thing? Prisons are the pits. The inmates who tell us they were glad they were in prison say so because God could never have gotten their attention on the outside. They had to be in a crisis situation, and everyone in prison is in crisis. Most inmates are desperate, divorced, disengaged, disenfranchised, disillusioned, dehumanized, depressed and despondent. Trauma, losses, horrible news, and bottomless pit situations put all of us in perilous predicaments. They have hit bottom! The only way to look is up.

God uses these experiences to make us think and grasp onto something. A great number of folks in and out of prisons have sought God in these times. Even in our darkest hour, God always breaks through with His brightest hope, Jesus. He is always there for us!

". . . lo I am with you always, even unto the end of the age."   Matthew 28:20

". . . I will never leave you nor forsake you."
                                                            Hebrews 13:5

YOU GO FIRST

Some years ago during a Weekend of Champions, Bunny Martin, Ron Kuntz, and I did a program on a women's death row. Two of the four women inmates had poisoned their husbands. All seemed to go well and, after our performance, we were invited to stay and help celebrate a birthday of one of the women. Some of the women correctional officers were also in attendance.

They served cookies, butterscotch pudding and coffee. I really like butterscotch pudding, but I was a little apprehensive. I asked who had made the pudding. The answer to my question further worried me. I said to the pudding maker, "You go first and I will eat some too." Laughter ensued, and a good time was had by all. All four of these women were now professing Christians. We assured them that we would dine with them again at The Wedding Feast in Glory!

DONALD LYKINS
(Best Friend)

In 1957 I met a successful businessman from Paris, Ky., named Donald Oscar Lykins; he became a real pest to me. We played golf. I wanted him to gamble, he would not. He wanted to speak of his faith. I would not listen. He visited Betty and me, and I still would not listen. On one occasion I met him at the door and told him he could come in, but he would have to leave the Bible stuff outside. He was hard to dissuade. He reminded me of a chicken after a Junebug. Insults rolled off him like water off a Duck's back. He never gave up. Jesus doesn't give up either!

Immediately after the Lord "arrested" me, Donald and I became great friends. I, like so many other new Christians, needed one great friend on the outside. My best friend Jesus was on the inside. Donald was a confidant, father image, counselor and mentor all rolled into one. He "Stayed the course" with me. Thank you Donald.

He told me the best thing I ever did for him was introducing him to the Prison Ministry. He said, "You bugged me until I went." He never stopped going! He virtually used up his remaining years serving the Lord in Prison Work.

Jane, his lovely bride of almost 60 years, was his constant companion and helper. She also is a fabulous cake maker. The platform guests will attest to this.

We had a wonderful time at his home going funeral. It truly was a praise and worship service. Jane said, "I know

Donald is pleased."

Mary Magdalene and Donald had a lot in common. Mary used up her expensive ointment to bathe Jesus feet. Jesus said of her, "SHE DID WHAT SHE COULD." Donald, "DID WHAT HE COULD!"

Donald was a diamond in the rough; yea, a "gem". Donald was a gracious, generous, gifted, God-honoring guy. He was my best buddy.

I feel very comfortable and pleased to know that Donald is saving me a place at the back of the table of the Wedding Feast. This will enable us to help to serve the coffee. Thank you, thank you, my dear friend!

GEORGE JOSLIN

Giants don't always have to be big and tough. George Joslin was only 5'3" and 120 pounds and a young 75 years of age. George reminded one of a little Bantam rooster. George was a giant in God's Kingdom. George was always suited up with a tie and a cocky little hat. It matched George. Once on a questionnaire that asked for his address and his zip, he quickly wrote, "You bet." I overheard and saw a beautiful scene with George and a very tall young African-American inmate. The inmate said, "Old man, you're bugging me. I could hit you on top of the head and drive you into the ground." George said, "That would be o.k., I'd be with Jesus. But let me tell you something first. Jesus loves you and I love you." This seemed to work, because in a little while, the big fellow was gloriously saved.

I have quite a few cherished letters from my dear departed friend, George. They are priceless. The beautiful grace-filled memory of George will forever be a part of the prison ministry. You see, George was a true Champion for Christ!

CAN'T GO HOME AGAIN

After attending a "Weekend of Champions" you truly can't go home again. The emphasis here is on "you." An old Indian chief said it well, "You can't put your moccasins in the same stream twice."

After a prison weekend, a different you, a changed you returns home. Nearly all the teammates relate that they are more compassionate, more sensitive to others' needs, and more eager to help. Most of us learn something about the real meaning of empathy – "sympathy on a two-way street."

Sometimes we get a taste of being Christ-like. Just like Jesus, we become blinded to the barriers. Barriers are what separate us from others. Love across the barriers is hard, especially if we are more concerned about the barriers than we are the people.

All who knew Dick Stump can never forget him. Dick was a successful insurance salesman from Indianapolis. He attended a Weekend of Champions. He went back home and shared Christ with everyone who did business with him. He led over a hundred folks to Jesus the first year. Quite frankly, there are many Dick Stumps in the prison ministry.

If anyone is interested in being a better mate, a better parent, a better neighbor, a better church member, or even a better citizen then you are more than welcome to be a part of a Weekend of Champions. But be apprised, "You can't go home again."

HEROES OF FAITH

In God's Book, and more specifically, the eleventh chapter of Hebrews, we find some Heroes of Faith. They assuredly understood that, "Without faith it is impossible to please God."

Gems for the Journey would like to submit a few Heroes of Faith who had faith to spare. They had so much that they had to share, and share they did! These heroes were an integral part of "Weekend of Champions."

It was Albert McMakin who took Billy Graham to the tent revival of Mordeci Ham, where Billy surrendered to God. Albert taught, all who would listen, many truths about our Lord. He also taught some of us about "So tales."

Carl and Mable Hamblen, Dick Stump, Dick Roher, Hazel Wilson, Ed Kilby, Larry Cowart, Ron Westmoreland, Ted Blake, George Joslin, Waddy Spoelstra, Donald Lykins and many others have gone home, "To be with Jesus Forever!" Newspaper accounts said they had died! No, no, no, they are more alive now! They merely changed addresses.

All of the above merely, "Did what they could!" They could do no more. They were Champions for Life and Champions for Eternity. They were "Gems" for us and they are "Gems" for Heaven. Could anyone imagine such a glorious exhilarating celebration! Praise The Lord!

"No good thing will He withhold from them who walk uprightly".   Psalm 94:11

THE FINEST HOUR

A Christian's finest hour at the

End of his road, his greatest

Fulfillment of all he holds dear

Is

That moment when he has

Worked his heart out in the good

And glorious cause of Christ and

Lies exhausted on the field of

Battle –

Victorious!

Bob Cole
Author

INEFFABLE TETRA GRAMMATON

Since you have read this far, it's time to reveal the meaning. There are not too many clues. Not like when Jesus asked His disciples, "Who do men say that I am?" He answered for them when He said, "I Am." This is the same "I Am" of the burning bush fame.

But, back to ineffable tetra grammaton. Ineffable means too wonderful to hear, too marvelous to touch, too holy to see. Tetra means four. Grammaton means letters of a noun. Altogether the meaning is the four letters (consonants) of the transliterated word "Yahweh" (Jehovah). The high priest only once a year and then only he could say Y.H.W.H. is the ineffable tetra grammaton.

"Yahweh" (Jehovah).

Thank God the veil was rent from top to bottom!

ENOUGH IS ENOUGH

My readers are saying, "Bob, you leave a lot of gaps. You leave a lot of things unsaid, but always implied. You have a lot of redundancy". I agree totally.

You can fill in the gaps. You can put flesh on the bones. You can complete the implications. Add your own companion scriptures. Make your own stories and sermons. Be my guest, but do it all for His Glory! Remember the most precious "Gem" of all is "The Pearl of Great Price"!

May God richly bless you and yours over and over, because He Forever Lives and So Will We.

In His Love,
Bob Cole

P.S. Keep the Faith, Baby
     Not the Baby Faith

<u>VISIT US ON OUR</u>
<u>WEB SITE:</u>

www.gemsforthejourney.com

<u>ORDERING INFORMATION:</u>

Info@gemsforthejourney.com